animate
FAITH

ILLUSTRATED BY
PAUL SOUPISET

WRITTEN BY
DR. ALLEN HILTON
& CARLA BARNHILL

SPARK
HOUSE | MINNEAPOLIS, MN

CONTRIBUTORS
NADIA BOLZ-WEBER, LILLIAN DANIEL, SHANE HIPPS, BRAIN MCLAREN, BRUCE REYES-CHOW, MARK SCANDRETTE, LAUREN WINNER

FACILITATOR GUIDE ILLUSTRATION
PAUL SOUPISET, WITH ADDITIONAL ILLUSTRATION BY MARK GUTIERREZ FOR TOOLBOX STUDIOS, INC.

FACILITATOR BOOK WRITER
DR. ALLEN HILTON, CARLA BARNHILL

SPARKHOUSE TEAM
ANDREW DEYOUNG, SUE HINTON, TONY JONES, JIM KAST-KEAT, TIMOTHY PAULSON, DAVID SCHOENKNECHT, KRISTOFER SKRADE

TOOLBOX STUDIOS TEAM
PAUL SOUPISET, MARK GUTIERREZ, BRET REPKA, STACY THOMAS, GABRIEL PARDO

VIDEO TEAM
KYLE ISENHOWER OF ISENHOWER PRODUCTIONS, SHANE NELSON OF OMNI-FUSION MEDIA PRODUCTION, SILAS KINDY OF ONE LIGHT COLLECTIVE

EDITORIAL TEAM
ERIN DAVIS

SPECIAL THANKS TO TYPESETTER SARAH FRANKEN AND PHOTOGRAPHER COURTNEY PERRY

THE PAPER USED IN THIS PUBLICATION MEETS THE MINIMUM REQUIREMENTS OF AMERICAN NATIONAL STANDARD FOR INFORMATION SCIENCES — PERMANENCE OF PAPER FOR PRINTED LIBRARY MATERIALS, ANSI Z329 . 48 -1984

MANUFACTURED IN THE U.S.A.

16   5 6 7 8 9 10

ISBN 978-1-4514-3083-7

COPYRIGHT © 2012

animate

FAITH

ONE LOOK AT THE MATERIALS FOR ANIMATE™ AND IT'S CLEAR THAT THIS IS SOMETHING...DIFFERENT.

BUT IT'S NOT JUST THE LOOKS OF THE ILLUSTRATED JOURNAL OR THE ANIMATED VIDEOS THAT MAKE THE ANIMATE™ SERIES UNIQUE. IT'S THE WAY WE HOPE YOU'LL USE THEM AND THE WAY WE BELIEVE THEY WILL CHANGE THE PEOPLE INVOLVED. THESE SESSIONS AREN'T MEANT TO BE LESSONS. THEY AREN'T MEANT TO PROVIDE ANSWERS. THEY AREN'T MEANT TO FIT NEATLY INTO SEVEN WEEKS AND THEN BE FORGOTTEN. NO, THESE SESSIONS ARE DESIGNED TO RAISE QUESTIONS, TO FLIP ESTABLISHED ANSWERS AND ASSUMPTIONS UPSIDE DOWN, TO STICK IN THE HEADS OF PARTICIPANTS FOR MONTHS AND EVEN YEARS TO COME.

WE KNOW THAT'S WHAT YOU'RE HOPING FOR, TOO. SO WE'VE PUT TOGETHER THIS FACILITATOR GUIDE TO HELP YOU MAKE THE MOST OUT OF THE VIDEOS AND THE JOURNAL. AS YOU FAMILIARIZE YOURSELF WITH THESE MATERIALS, THERE ARE A FEW THINGS TO KEEP IN MIND:

1) THIS IS YOUR EXPERIENCE AND NO ONE WILL UNDERSTAND THE DYNAMICS OF YOUR GROUP LIKE YOU DO.

SO WHILE WE'VE DEVELOPED GROUP ACTIVITIES AND SUGGESTED DISCUSSION QUESTIONS AND PULLED AT THREADS IN THE VIDEOS THAT SEEM COMPELLING, WE WANT YOU TO TAKE THIS STUFF AND RUN WITH IT. MAKE IT WORK FOR YOUR GROUP. IGNORE ACTIVITIES THAT DON'T FIT YOUR PEOPLE. IF THE VIDEOS AND SKETCHES SUGGEST ALTERNATIVE QUESTIONS THAT ARE CRUCIAL TO YOUR COMMUNITY, GO WITH IT.

2) THE RIGHT SIDE OF YOUR BRAIN IS ABOUT TO GET A WORKOUT.

THOSE OF US WHO FIND OURSELVES IN LEADERSHIP POSITIONS TEND TO BE LEFT BRAIN TYPES—WE LIKE ANSWERS, WE LIKE ORDER, WE LIKE PROBLEMS WE CAN SOLVE. BUT THE ANIMATE™ SERIES IS MEANT TO BE CREATIVE AND USER-GENERATED. YOU'LL FIND THAT THE JOURNALS AREN'T WRITTEN TRANSCRIPTS OF THE VIDEOS—SOMETIMES THE JOURNAL CONTENT WILL ONLY HINT AT THE SPEAKER'S WORDS. THE GRAPHICS IN THE JOURNAL DON'T ALWAYS READ FROM LEFT TO RIGHT OR TOP TO BOTTOM. THE SUGGESTIONS IN THIS GUIDE WON'T ALWAYS HAVE A DIRECT CONNECTION TO THE SESSION CONTENT. THIS OPEN-ENDED APPROACH IS INTENDED TO INVITE PARTICIPANTS TO SHARE THEIR QUESTIONS, EXPERIENCES, AND OPINIONS IN AN OPEN-SOURCE ENVIRONMENT.

3) YOU DON'T HAVE TO KNOW EVERYTHING.

THE ANIMATE™ SERIES IS DESIGNED TO BE A JUMPING OFF POINT, NOT THE END POINT. IF QUESTIONS COME UP THAT YOU AREN'T READY FOR, THAT'S OKAY. YOU DON'T HAVE TO BE THE EXPERT. NATURALLY YOU NEED TO BE FAMILIAR WITH EACH VIDEO BEFORE THE SESSION, BUT YOU DON'T HAVE TO AGREE WITH EVERYTHING THE SPEAKERS SAY OR UNDERSTAND EVERY IDEA THEY THROW OUT. SO LET THEIR THOUGHTS SPARK CONVERSATION AND SEE WHERE IT TAKES THE GROUP. PART OF THIS EXPERIENCE IS JOINING IN WITH YOUR GROUP AS YOU EXPLORE THESE IDEAS TOGETHER.

4) CONSIDER THE ROLE OF SOCIAL MEDIA.

THE IDEAS IN THESE SESSIONS ARE MEATY AND THERE'S FAR MORE TO THINK ABOUT AND DISCUSS THAN YOU'LL BE ABLE TO FIT INTO AN HOUR-LONG SESSION. SO THINK ABOUT WAYS TO USE SOCIAL MEDIA OR OTHER EASY-TO-ACCESS ONLINE TOOLS TO FACILITATE CONVERSATION DURING THE WEEK. YOU COULD SET UP A FACEBOOK GROUP, DESIGNATE A TWITTER HASHTAG, OR PUT TOGETHER A GOOGLE DOC FOR POSTING THOUGHTS AND QUESTIONS. IF THIS ISN'T YOUR STYLE, LET THE GROUP COME UP WITH WAYS TO STAY CONNECTED BETWEEN SESSIONS.

THE ANIMATE | FAITH SESSIONS ARE LIKE A GUIDED TOUR THROUGH THE BASICS OF CHRISTIAN THEOLOGY. AND YOU'RE IN GOOD HANDS—BRIAN MCLAREN, NADIA BOLZ-WEBER, SHANE HIPPS, LILLIAN DANIEL, LAUREN WINNER, BRUCE REYES-CHOW, MARK SCANDRETTE. THESE MEN AND WOMEN BRING YOU THEIR YEARS OF EXPERIENCE, BUT MORE IMPORTANTLY, THEY BRING YOU THEIR QUESTIONS, THEIR WONDERINGS, AND THEIR EXPERIENCES OF TRAVELING THIS OFTEN-BUMPY ROAD OF FAITH.

YOUR ROLE IS TO BE THE GUIDE WHO BRINGS YOUR GROUP TO A GALLERY OF IDEAS, SHOWS THEM AROUND A BIT, THEN LETS THEM WANDER AROUND WHILE THEY SPEND TIME WITH THOSE THAT COMPEL THEM MOST. IT WILL BE AN ANIMATING EXPERIENCE—FOR ALL OF YOU.

How about a quick tour of a typical session? As you can see, nearly every spread in the Journal is packed with graphic elements. Until participants get used to the idea that this journal is meant to be messed with, they might be overwhelmed by all the words and images. This Facilitator Guide will help you navigate the sessions and bring the conversation to life.

Group Activities:
These activities range from ice-breakers to discussion questions to follow-up activities. You can use all of them, one or two of them, or none of them. Once you get a feel for how your group's time will flow, you'll have a better sense of how many of these you want to use in a given session.

CONNECTIONS: CONSIDER THE DOTTED LINES YOUR TRAIL MAP THAT SHOWS THE CONNECTIONS BETWEEN THE FACILITATOR'S CONTENT AND THE JOURNAL CONTENT OR EVEN BETWEEN RELATED IDEAS. FEEL FREE TO ADD SOME LINES OF YOUR OWN!

LEADER TIPS:
Asterisks mark where you'll find suggestions for props, background music, and additional materials to have on hand for each session. You'll also want to raid your church's art supplies for colored pencils, crayons, markers, or other supplies that will encourage participants to add their own words and images to their journals.

FACTOIDS: TO SAVE YOU SOME HOMEWORK, WE'VE INCLUDED A FEW BACKGROUND NOTES THAT HELP ILLUSTRATE A POINT IN THE SESSION OR DRAW OUT SOME OF THE HISTORY BEHIND THE CONVERSATION.

QUOTES: EACH OF THE SESSION PRESENTERS ARE HIGHLY QUOTABLE. BUT WE'VE HIGHLIGHTED SOME OF THEIR BEST STUFF TO GIVE YOU A FEW JUMPING-OFF POINTS AS YOU WEAVE THE VIDEOS INTO YOUR CONVERSATIONS. OH, AND THERE'S AN OCCASIONAL QUOTE FROM A FEW OTHERS AS WELL.

Scholarly Footnotes: These notes offer more advanced background to the content. Use them to prepare for a session or as a way to follow up sessions with additional resources.

TO MAKE THE MOST OF EACH SESSION,

we suggest starting with a short (like 10 minutes or so) recap of the previous session and any between-session research or reflection that group may have done. You may want to take a little time to also ask about any prior knowledge or experience participants may have regarding the topic of the day.

THE VIDEO IS A KEY ELEMENT OF

animate™. By way of it, your group gets to sit at the feet of some of the 21st century's most fascinating scholars and practitioners of the Christian faith. While these folks may be unknown to the members of your group, they are among the thought leaders of today's church. When exactly you show the video is kind of up to you, but getting to know the presenters ahead of time could be helpful to your group.

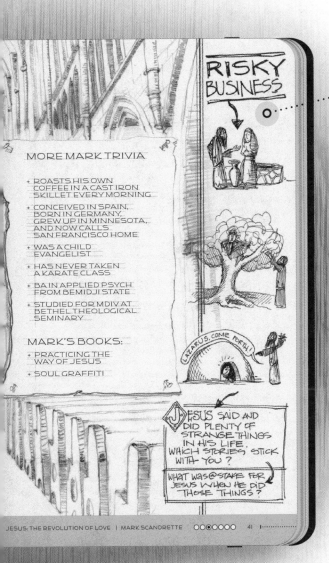

RISKY BUSINESS

MORE MARK TRIVIA

+ ROASTS HIS OWN COFFEE IN A CAST IRON SKILLET EVERY MORNING
+ CONCEIVED IN SPAIN, BORN IN GERMANY, GREW UP IN MINNESOTA, AND NOW CALLS SAN FRANCISCO HOME
+ WAS A CHILD EVANGELIST
+ HAS NEVER TAKEN A KARATE CLASS
+ BA IN APPLIED PSYCH FROM BEMIDJI STATE
+ STUDIED FOR MDIV AT BETHEL THEOLOGICAL SEMINARY

MARK'S BOOKS:

+ PRACTICING THE WAY OF JESUS
+ SOUL GRAFFITI

LAZARUS, COME FORTH!

JESUS SAID AND DID PLENTY OF STRANGE THINGS IN HIS LIFE. WHICH STORIES STICK WITH YOU?

WHAT WAS @ STAKE FOR JESUS WHEN HE DID THOSE THINGS?

JESUS: THE REVOLUTION OF LOVE | MARK SCANDRETTE ○○◉○○○○ 41

These sessions are meant to be a bit provocative, so you'll also find ideas for dealing with the frustrations that can come with challenging deep-seated beliefs. Ask the questions provided. Add a few of your own. But give the group time to breathe—to sketch, to write, to pray, to engage with their Journals and each other.

FACTOIDS ALSO PROVIDE SUGGESTIONS FOR ADDITIONAL READING OR PROVIDE OTHER RESOURCES FOR THOSE WHO WANT TO DIG DEEPER.

Make sure that you save at least one of these activities for participants to explore outside of class, either on their own or through social media conversations with others.

 – GROUP ACTIVITIES WITH QUESTIONS DESIGNED TO HELP ANIMATE CONVERSATION.

{ } – INTRODUCTORY AND OUT-GOING THOUGHTS TO SET-UP THE SESSION AND TO KEEP INTERACTIONS GOING BETWEEN SESSIONS.

* – LEADER TIPS: IDEAS TO HELP FACILITATORS FACILITATE.

! – FACTOIDS: INFORMATIONAL TIDBITS TO SPICE UP THE CONVERSATION.

" " – QUOTES FROM THE VIDEO AND ELSEWHERE TO GET FOLKS THINKING.

| · 〉 – FOOTNOTES: EXTRA BACKGROUND MATERIAL TO MAKE YOU SOUND EVEN SMARTER.

The introductory and out-going content for each session—as indicated by the parentheses icons—are not meant to contain the session, but to provide a space for it to be experienced as a group. Use the prompts in out-going content to challenge your group to apply their animate™ conversations to life.

FAITH – AT A GLANCE

GOD | BRIAN: "IF YOU ASK ME, 'IS GOD REAL?' I FIRST HAVE TO ASK, 'WHICH GOD ARE WE TALKING ABOUT?'" WITH THESE WORDS, BRIAN MCLAREN GIVES VOICE TO A COMMON STRUGGLE AMONG PEOPLE OF FAITH—WHO EXACTLY IS THIS GOD WE WORSHIP? IS GOD A MIGHTY FORTRESS, SOLID AND UNCHANGING? IS GOD A MYSTICAL, UNKNOWABLE FORCE THAT FLOATS AROUND US LIKE A VAPOR? HOW CAN WE SPEAK OF FAITH IF WE CAN'T EVEN SPEAK OF GOD WITH ANY CERTAINTY? HOW CAN WE CHART A COURSE THROUGH THE OFTEN-MURKY WATERS OF CHRISTIAN TRADITION AND FIND OUR WAY TO GOD?

RELIGION | LILLIAN: WHAT DOES IT MEAN TO BE SPIRITUAL? IS IT THE SAME AS BEING RELIGIOUS? LILLIAN DANIEL PUSHES BACK AT THIS QUESTION THAT HAS BEEN STIRRING UP THE CULTURAL CONVERSATION FOR A WHILE NOW. SHE ASKS US TO CONSIDER HOW THE SEEDS OF FAITH TAKE ROOT AND THRIVE. WHAT ROLE DOES ORGANIZED RELIGION PLAY IN HELPING—OR HINDERING—GROWTH? IF RELIGION IS THE PROBLEM, WHY HAS IT HELD FAST FOR THOUSANDS OF YEARS? IN THIS AGE OF RELIGIOUS PLURALISM, IS IT POSSIBLE OR EVEN DESIRABLE TO STICK WITH OUR AGE-OLD TRADITIONS?

JESUS | MARK: WHAT DOES IT MEAN TO WALK IN THE WAY OF JESUS? TO EXPLORE THIS QUESTION, MARK SCANDRETTE LOOKS TO THE ANCIENT JAPANESE CONCEPT OF THE DOJO. WHAT IF OUR CHURCHES BECAME PLACES WHERE WE PRACTICED BEING LIKE JESUS? WHAT IF WE WERE SERIOUS ABOUT JOINING IN WITH JESUS' REVOLUTION OF LOVE? WHAT IF WE TOOK THE KIND OF SOCIAL AND ECONOMIC RISKS JESUS TOOK AND RESHAPED WHAT IT MEANS TO BE A CHRISTIAN? AS MARK INVITES US INTO THE DOJO, WE FIND OURSELVES LOOKING AT A MASTER WHO MIGHT BE ASKING US TO WALK DOWN A PATH WE NEVER IMAGINED.

SALVATION | SHANE: THE CROSS OF CHRIST STANDS AS A SYMBOL OF GOD'S SAVING WORK. BUT WHAT, EXACTLY, DOES IT MEAN TO BE SAVED? FROM WHAT? FOR WHAT? IS SALVATION A REWARD WE CLAIM AT DEATH OR SOMETHING MEANT TO CHANGE OUR LIVES RIGHT NOW? FOR SHANE HIPPS, THESE ARE THE QUESTIONS WE NEED TO ANSWER IF WE ARE TO TRULY RECEIVE THE RELEASE THAT COMES WITH SALVATION IN THE HERE AND NOW.

CROSS | NADIA: THE CROSS SITS AT THE CENTER OF OUR FAITH, AND YET OUR UNDERSTANDING OF WHAT EXACTLY HAPPENED ON THAT CROSS REMAINS CONFLICTED AND CONFUSING. WAS JESUS OUR PROXY? THE PAYMENT? THE ONLY WAY TO APPEASE AN ANGRY GOD? NADIA BOLZ-WEBER REMINDS US THAT OUR THEORIES ABOUT THE CROSS TELL US AS MUCH ABOUT OURSELVES AND OUR VIEW OF GOD AS THEY DO ABOUT JESUS AND SALVATION.

BIBLE | LAUREN: WHY READ THE BIBLE? THIS IS LAUREN WINNER'S CENTRAL QUESTION. FOR LAUREN, AN AVID READER, THERE REMAINS SOMETHING ODD ABOUT THE WAY CHRISTIANS READ THE BIBLE. WHY DO WE KEEP TURNING TO THE SAME STORIES IN SEARCH OF SOME NEW REVELATION? WHAT IS IT ABOUT THE BIBLE THAT MAKES IT WORTH REPEATED READING? WHAT GETS IN OUR WAY AS WE READ THE BIBLE AND TRY TO MAKE SENSE OF IT? THESE ARE ISSUES THE CHURCH HAS WRESTLED WITH FOR CENTURIES AND YET WE KEEP AT IT. WE KEEP COMING BACK TO THIS BOOK AND ITS STRANGE NARRATIVE FULL OF PLAGUES AND MIRACLES AND DESTRUCTION AND REBIRTH. SO WHY DO WE DO IT?

CHURCH | BRUCE: BRUCE REYES-CHOW KNOWS HE'S NOT INVENTING THE METAPHOR OF THE CHURCH AS FAMILY. SO HE SUGGESTS WE TAKE OUR CHANGING NOTIONS ABOUT WHAT IT MEANS TO BE A FAMILY AND LET THEM SEEP INTO OUR UNDERSTANDING OF THE CHURCH. FOR BRUCE, IT'S THE MESSINESS, THE DYSFUNCTION, AND THE JOY THAT COMES FROM COMPLEX RELATIONSHIPS THAT MAKE CHURCH WORTH HANGING ON TO. SO HOW DO WE STAY CONNECTED TO THIS SOMETIMES-BROKEN FAMILY SYSTEM? WHAT DOES IT MEAN TO COMMIT OURSELVES TO THE CHURCH FAMILY, FOR BETTER OR FOR WORSE?

GOD | FAITH IS A QUEST
BRIAN MCLAREN

HOW ARE YOU EMBARKED ON A JOURNEY OF
SEEKING FOR GOD AND KEEPING THE QUEST ALIVE?

Welcome to Animate! You're about to embark on a journey of faith with the help of seven gifted and unique twenty-first century theologians. First up, Brian McLaren exposes our inability to fully comprehend God. He reveals the dangers of our suppositions and helps us to plot a course between them as we continue our quest for and with God.

PLAY SOME MUSIC

that gets people thinking outside the box about God such as "Magnificent" by U2 or the hymn "Immortal, Invisible, God Only Wise." Set the room with widely differing images of God. Encourage group members to consider these images as they arrive.

ANIMATE IS ALL ABOUT

having animated conversations about faith. If this is the first time your group has met, begin with an icebreaker game or a question everyone can answer about him or herself. As the sense of community develops people will feel free to be themselves.

WHO IS Brian McLAREN

BRIAN McLAREN GRABBE THE ATTENTION OF DISENCHANTED CHRISTIAN WITH HIS BOOK A NEW KIND OF CHRISTIAN (2001). LATER, IN 2005, HE WAS NAMED ONE OF TIME MAGAZINE'S 25 MOST INFLUENTIAL EVANGELICALS IN AMERIC. BRIAN'S INFLUENCE HAS BEEN THE RESULT OF HIS WILLINGNESS TO ADMIT THAT HE ISN'T ALWAYS SURE ABOUT HIS FAITH AND THAT HE USUALLY HAS FAR MORE QUESTION THAN ANSWERS.

MORE BRIAN TRIVIA:
- BRIAN WAS A COLLEGE ENGLISH PROFESSOR WHEN HE AND HIS WIFE STARTED A CHURCH IN THEIR LIVING ROOM.
- THAT CHURCH BECAME CEDAR RIDGE COMMUNITY CHURCH AND BRIAN WAS THEIR PASTOR FOR NEARLY 20 YEARS.
- LIVES ON MARCO ISLAND IN FLORIDA WHERE HE RAISES DOZENS OF EXOTIC TORTOISES IN HIS BACKYARD
- RELEASED AN ALBUM OF ORIGINAL MUSIC CALLED "LEARNING HOW TO LOVE" IN 1978.
- BA AND MA IN ENGLISH FROM UNIVERSITY OF MARYLAND

BRIAN'S BOOKS:
- A NEW KIND OF CHRISTIAN
- A GENEROUS ORTHODOXY
- EVERYTHING MUST CHANGE
- NAKED SPIRITUALITY

animate | 8

Brian McLaren has been a source of inspiration for "disenchanted Christians." Read through his bio and the quote together.
• When have you felt "disenchanted" with your faith? What brought you back?
• An old English mapmaker penned the phrase "here be dragons" at the edges of the known world. When it comes to God—what enchants you most, the known or the unknown?
• Read Isaiah 55 together then ask: What can you know about God? What remains unknown?

BRIAN McLAREN IS ONE OF THE UNOFFICIAL FOUNDERS OF WHAT HAS BECOME THE EMERGING CHURCH, A MOVEMENT OF CHURCHES THAT HAS VITALIZED AMERICAN CHRISTIANITY DURING THE 1990S AND 2000S BY TAKING THE POST-MODERN WORLD SERIOUSLY AS THEY IMAGINE GOD AND CHURCH.

Eddie Gibbs and Ryan Bolger hoped to define the movement in their book, *Emerging Churches: Creating Christian Community in Postmodern Cultures* (Grand Rapids, Mich.: Baker Academic, 2005). A notorious critique of Brian McLaren's way of thinking of God is D. A. Carson's *Becoming Conversant with the Emerging Church* (Grand Rapids, Mich: Zondervan, 2005).

Scot McKnight breaks through stereotypes in his article, "Five Streams of the Emerging Church: Key elements of the most controversial and misunderstood movement in the church today," *Christianity Today*, Feb 2007. (http://www.christianitytoday.com/ct/2007/february/11.35.html)

SOMETIMES, WHEN I HEAR PEOPLE SPEAK ABOUT GOD, I FEEL LIKE AN ATHEIST. THE GOD THEY SPEAK OF I DON'T BELIEVE IN: A GOD WHO LOVES CHRISTIANS BUT HATES MUSLIMS; OR A GOD WHO POURS LUXURIES ON THE RICH BUT CONSIGNS THE POOR TO POVERTY; OR A GOD WHO CARES ABOUT HUMAN SOULS BUT DOESN'T CARE ABOUT CONSERVING AND PROTECTING OUR BEAUTIFUL, FRAGILE PLANET. SO IF YOU ASK ME, "IS GOD REAL?" I FIRST HAVE TO ASK, "WHICH GOD ARE WE TALKING ABOUT? AND WHAT DO YOU MEAN BY GOD?"

—BRIAN MCLAREN

WHAT IMAGES OF GOD HAVE YOU LET GO OF?

WHAT IMAGES OF GOD RESONATE WITH YOU?

GOD: FAITH IS A QUEST | BRIAN MCLAREN   9

Invite people to share images and pictures of God they've seen throughout their lives. Out loud or in their Journals, have them describe or sketch their own thoughts about how they picture God. Encourage your group to come up with their own picture of God without regard for a "right" answer. Brian confesses that sometimes he feels like an atheist when he hears other people talk about God.
• What confessions could you make about your beliefs about God?
• How has your image of God changed and developed throughout your life?
• What images of God have you let go of?
• What images of God resonate with you?

SCATTERED THROUGHOUT THIS

session is art that's suggestive of things needed to repair a sailing vessel, even while underway if need be. More than just keeping Christianity afloat, Brian has given his life to helping Christians reach beyond the horizons of what they've always believed about their faith.

Where do we get our God? Here's a study of how young children "inherit" their view of God from their context: "Young Children's Descriptions of God: Influences of parents' and teachers' God concepts and religious denomination of schools," in *Journal of Beliefs & Values: Studies in Religion & Education*, Vol 22, Issue 1, 2001.

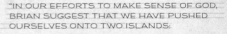

"IF FORTRESS PEOPLE REDUCE GOD TO CONCRETE FACTS, CLOUD PEOPLE REDUCE GOD TO FOGGY OPINIONS. IF FORTRESS PEOPLE TURN FAITH INTO A VICIOUS FIGHT ABOUT WHO'S MORE RIGHT, CLOUD PEOPLE REDUCE FAITH TO A KIND OF INCONSEQUENTIAL LEISURE ACTIVITY, LIKE DOING CROSSWORD PUZZLES OR COLLECTING REFRIGERATOR MAGNETS OR BEING WINE CONNOISSEURS."

IT WILL ALWAYS HELP YOU TO WATCH

the video once or twice in advance to develop your own thoughts and questions. As you listen to Brian, consider your group's theological range. Will any feel like the villains in Brian's presentation? Position Brian (as well as the other animate theologians throughout this course) as a helpful contributor to your conversation but not as the last word.

Watch the video together.
• What inspired you in the video? What challenged you? What concerned you?
• When have you been able to relate to Brian's frustration: that the God he hears about from some Christians is NOT a God he believes in?
• Do you feel more like a Fortress of Certainty person or a Castle of Opinions person? Describe.

"IN OUR EFFORTS TO MAKE SENSE OF GOD, BRIAN SUGGEST THAT WE HAVE PUSHED OURSELVES ONTO TWO ISLANDS:

ON ONE, WE GATHER AROUND AN IMAGE OF GOD AS A FORTRESS, OUR STRENGTH AND SHIELD. GOD IS OUR ROCK—SOLID, UNCHANGING, STEADY.

ON THE OTHER, WE FIND OURSELVES HOVERING AROUND A FLOATING CASTLE ON A CLOUD, WHERE GO IS FOGGY AND SPECULATIVE. GOD IS EVERYWHERE AND NOWHERE. GOD IS UNKNOWABLE, MYSTICAL, AND FAR OUTSIDE OF HUMAN EXPERIENCE."

CERTITUDE

animate

Brian helps us map our theological territory by providing two extremes—absolute certainty and total relativism. In their Journals, have group members mark where their beliefs lie between the islands. Perhaps they're solidly on one side or another. Perhaps they've gone back and forth throughout their lives. Perhaps they're stuck on the island in the middle or even sailing off into the horizon.
• What are the benefits of having beliefs about God that are absolutely certain? What are the drawbacks?
• What are the benefits and drawbacks of having beliefs that are entirely relative and theoretical?
• Where did you mark yourself on this spread? Why?

"THE IDEA OF THE TRINITY, SO CENTRAL TO TRADITIONAL CHRISTIAN UNDERSTANDINGS OF GOD, TAKES A GREAT DEAL OF IMAGINATION. THROUGH HISTORY, PEOPLE HAVE USED IMAGES LIKE THREE DANCERS MOVING IN A CIRCLE, OR THREE LEAVES OF A CLOVER, OR THREE STATES OF WATER TO TRY TO CONVEY THAT ONE GOD CAN EXIST IN THREE PERSONS OR THAT THREE PERSONS CAN CONSTITUTE ONE GOD."

THE TRINITY IS A GREAT EXAMPLE OF HOW COMPLICATED IT CAN BE TO ANSWER THE QUESTION "WHO IS GOD?"

THE DOCTRINE OF THE TRINITY ISN'T REALLY IN THE BIBLE—THERE WE FIND THE SEEDS IF THIS IDEA. BUT EARLY CHRISTIANS NEEDED WAYS TO TALK ABOUT GOD BEING THE BABY IN THE MANGER, THE BREATH OF LIFE, AND THE CREATOR OF THE UNIVERSE.

BY THE 5TH CENTURY, WE HAD A DOCTRINE OF THE TRINITY, BUT IT'S A CONCEPT MANY OF US STILL HAVE A HARD TIME UNDERSTANDING.

GOD: FAITH IS A QUEST. | BRIAN MCLAREN.

In the video Brian uses the doctrine of the Trinity as an example of how complicated it can be to answer the question, "Who is God?" Invite group members to write the three persons of the Trinity at the points of the symbol in their Journals.
• How does this symbol represent how the Trinity is interconnected?
• How have you pictured the Trinity?
• What does the Trinity tell you about the nature of God?
• Can either castle claim that doctrine as its own? Why or why not?
• How would you describe to someone unfamiliar with the Trinity how God is three AND one?

Brian says that he feels like an atheist when he hears how some Christians describe God. (See the quote on the previous spread.) Bring in the atheist experience by engaging the ideas of people who do not believe in a god of any kind.
• What arguments have you heard against the existence of God?
• How do you react to those arguments?
• How do you process these ideas within your own beliefs about God?
• What argument would you make for the existence of God?

NEO-ATHEIST WRITERS LIKE SAM HARRIS, RICHARD DAWKINS, AND CHRISTOPHER HITCHENS HAVE ATTACKED BELIEF IN GOD ON THE GROUNDS THAT IT IS NOT COMPATIBLE WITH SCIENCE AND A MODERN WORLD-VIEW; AND THAT RELIGIOUS PEOPLE MAKE THE WORLD WORSE.

Sam Harris, *The End of Faith: Religion, Terror, and the Future of Reason* (New York: Norton, 2004); Richard Dawkins, *The God Delusion* (New York: Houghton-Mifflin, 2006); Christopher Hitchens, *God Is Not Great: How Religion Poisons Everything* (New York: Hachette, 2007).

Walk through the images of God in the Journal under "kataphasis." Have group members mark or cross out the images they see and don't see in their view of God. Then talk about the theological non-negotiables in your group. Invite group members to share one image, idea, or view of God that they won't concede. For example, "I can flex on a whole lots of things, but God as parent is most important to me." Have a volunteer write these non-negotiables on chart paper. Talk about how those different ideas can co-exist and work together in one faith.

KATAPHATIC THEOLOGY SEEKS TO UNDERSTAND GOD USING FAMILIAR IMAGES AS METAPHORS. IN BRIAN'S WORDS, "OUR IMAGES AND WORDS REALLY CAN HELP US TO CONCEIVE OF AND RELATE TO GOD."

THIS WOULD BE A GOOD TIME

to introduce Bible study tools like printed or online concordances, which are helpful in finding where exactly God is referred to as a "mother bear" for example. Note: Not all the images on this page are Biblical images.

What sketches don't seem to fit on this page? If you're thinking the coil of line and the cleat, then maybe the group ought to think again.
• What's the purpose of these items, nautically speaking?
• How does that fit in with your conversation about the images of God?
• Hebrews 6:19 uses similar imagery when describing what it's like to "look behind the curtain" between us and God.

"WHEN WE HOLD THESE TWO TRADITIONS IN PROPER BALANCE, WE KEEP SEEKING GOD, REACHING OUT TO GOD, AND RELATING TO GOD, ALWAYS REMEMBERING THAT GOD CAN NEVER BE FULLY GRASPED IN HAND OR CAPTURED IN A BOX OR STUFFED INTO THE HIP POCKET OF OUR TINY LITTLE MINDS."

APOPHATIC THEOLOGY (ALSO KNOWN AS THE *VIA NEGATIVA*) UNDERSTANDS GOD THROUGH THE SUBTRACTION OF IMAGES. IN BRIAN'S WORDS, "GOD CAN NEVER BE REDUCED TO IMAGES OR CONTAINED BY WORDS."

Have your group critique the claims they made when talking about their kataphatic views of God.
• How do your images fall short of the actual God?
• How do ALL images fall short?
• How does it help to know God is beyond your human imagination?

"FOR WE EXPLAIN NOT WHAT GOD IS BUT CANDIDLY CONFESS THAT WE HAVE NOT EXACT KNOWLEDGE CONCERNING HIM. FOR IN WHAT CONCERNS GOD TO CONFESS OUR IGNORANCE IS THE BEST KNOWLEDGE." (SAINT CYRIL OF JERUSALEM, IN HIS CATECHETICAL HOMILIES)

ἀπόφασις

Try the kataphatic-apophatic balance Brian suggests in the video. Look up the image of the nursing mother God in Isaiah 49:13-16.
• How does this metaphor help you understand and connect with God?
• What are the metaphor's limitations?
Next, follow Brian's lead: "[The insight of Apophatic Theology] means that reverent loving silence is sometimes the most eloquent form of theology." Take a moment for meditation. Consider lighting a candle as a focal point for your group.
• What did you discover in the silence?
• How has the indescribable God appeared in your life?

MEMBERS OF YOUR GROUP COULD

use this same approach on their own between sessions. On the kataphatic side, have them choose an image of God to do more research on, then report to the group by way of social networking or when the group comes back together. On the apophatic side, encourage them to make time for silence and meditation, emptying their mind to quest for God.

Contemporary theologians reflect on apophasis in, *Silence and the Word: Negative Theology and Incarnation*, ed. Davies and Turner (Cambridge Press, 2002).

"SOMETIMES I HAVE EXPERIENCED GOD IN EXTRAORDINARY WAYS—IN DRAMATIC SURPRISES OR SOUL-EXPANDING INSIGHTS OR UNEXPLAINABLE MYSTICAL ENCOUNTERS. MORE OFTEN, I HAVE FELTS GOD'S REALITY IN THE SIMPLE ENCOURAGEMENT OF A FRIEND, IN THE GENTLE INSPIRATION OF A SERMON, OR IN THE FAMILIAR RITUAL OF THE EUCHARIST. AND I'D BE LESS THAN HONEST IF I DIDN'T ALSO SAY THAT AT TIMES, I'VE FOUND MYSELF IN THE SPIRITUAL DOLDRUMS, CAST ADRIFT, WONDERING IF THE WIND WOULD EVER BLOW AGAIN."

THE LONG TITLE OF BRIAN'S BOOK REVEALS A LOT: A *GENEROUS ORTHODOXY: WHY I AM A MISSIONAL, EVANGELICAL, POST/PROTESTANT, LIBERAL/CONSERVATIVE, MYSTICAL/POETIC, BIBLICAL, CHARISMATIC/CONTEMPLATIVE, FUNDAMENTALIST/CALVINIST, ANABAPTIST/ANGLICAN, METHODIST, CATHOLIC, GREEN, INCARNATIONAL, DEPRESSED-YET-HOPEFUL, EMERGENT, UNFINISHED CHRISTIAN* (MINNEAPOLIS, MINN: YOUTH SPECIALTIES BOOKS, 2004).

Display the extended title of *A Generous Orthodoxy* so everyone can read it.
• How can a person be all those things?
• What does it look like to be a Liberal/ Conservative? Depressed-yet-Hopeful?
• To unpack the term "unfinished," read Philippians 1:6 and 2:12-13 together. How is *God* at work in you?

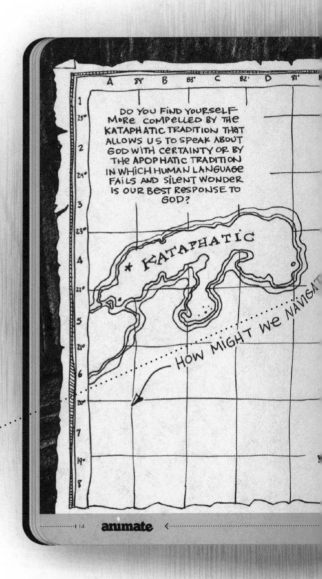

DO YOU FIND YOURSELF MORE COMPELLED BY THE KATAPHATIC TRADITION THAT ALLOWS US TO SPEAK ABOUT GOD WITH CERTAINTY OR BY THE APOPHATIC TRADITION IN WHICH HUMAN LANGUAGE FAILS AND SILENT WONDER IS OUR BEST RESPONSE TO GOD?

KATAPHATIC

HOW MIGHT WE NAVIGAT

animate

CONSIDER THE AMERICAN POLITICAL SCENE, WHERE EACH PARTY HAS A PASSIONATE AND CERTAIN (AND OFTEN EXTREME) "BASE." CHURCHES HAVE THAT DYNAMIC, TOO. IN HIS MINISTRY, BRIAN HAS HOPED TO DEFY THAT STEREOTYPE AND BRING OPPOSITES TOGETHER BY MARRYING GENEROSITY WITH ORTHODOXY.

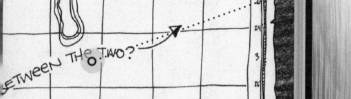

Take two minutes to brainstorm some faith practices members of your group have engaged. Have a volunteer write them on an enlarged version of the chart in the Journal. Mark practices as being more apophatic or kataphatic.
• How do your faith practices reveal how we view God?
• How do your faith practices contribute to our faith as a quest?
• How do you use your faith practices and other faith encounters to navigate between your kataphatic and apophatic self?

"IN BETWEEN THESE EXTREMES, THE REST OF US NEED A THIRD ALTERNATIVE. WE DON'T WANT FAITH TO BE A FIGHT, AND WE DON'T WANT FAITH TO BE A FOG. WE WANT OUR FAITH TO BE A QUEST: A QUEST FOR GOD, AND WITH GOD."

Have the group play with the chart. What course has their faith been on? Where would they draw dragons and other navigational hazards? Is it clear sailing with God for them, or has their faith been close to shipwreck a time or two? Perhaps they could even mark some things on the map that they treasure about God.

Select a few of the following scriptures and talk about how they serve as buoys or lighthouses along our faith quests.

Kataphatic Scriptures: Father (The Lord's Prayer in Matthew 6:9), a vintner (Isaiah 5:1-35); a husband (Jeremiah 3:31-34); a king (Revelation 4:1-11), a hen (Luke 13:34), and shepherd (Psalm 23).

Apophatic Scriptures: Romans 11:33-36, 1 Timothy 6:16; John 1:18.

Encourage members to share others that have offered significant guidance for their voyage to and with God.

"WHICH DO YOU SEE AS THE GREATER DANGER IN TODAY'S WORLD AND IN YOUR OWN LIFE: FAITH AS AN EMBATTLED FORTRESS OR FAITH AS A CASTLE UP IN THE CLOUDS?"

A more physical way to open this conversation is actually to put two stones (or things that looks like stones) out in the room representing Scylla and Charybdis. Picture one as a lock-down fortress and the other as an airy castle. Have your group walk the path toward or between these rocks. Then picture the other Scylla and Charybdis dynamics of your experienced faith life.

• What are the rocks we steer between? Are there other dangers?

• Is there anything that has helped or can help us steer clear?

• Whether you are talking a car or a ship, it's a lot easier to steer if you don't look right in front of you. What's on the horizon of your quest? Is God calling you toward some new direction?

HOMER MYTHOLOGIZED TWO NAVIGATIONAL HAZARDS, A WHIRLPOOL AND ROCKY SHOALS ON EITHER SIDE OF THE STRAIT BETWEEN ITALY AND THE ISLAND OF SICILY, AS A PAIR OF SEA MONSTERS THROUGH WHICH ODYSSEUS HAD TO PASS ON HIS QUEST. OVER TIME THE LATIN PROVERB, *INCIDIT IN SCYLLAM CUPIENS VITARE CHARYBDIM* (HE RUNS ON SCYLLA, WISHING TO AVOID CHARYBDIS), SPUN-OFF ENGLISH VARIATIONS LIKE "BETWEEN A ROCK AND A HARD PLACE" AND "BETWEEN THE DEVIL AND THE DEEP BLUE SEA"—ALL OF WHICH SERVE TO ILLUSTRATE A DIFFICULT, IF NOT IMPOSSIBLE, CHOICE. BUT IS CRASHING INTO ONE OR BEING CAPSIZED BY THE OTHER THE ONLY COURSE FOR CHRISTIANS WHEN IT COMES TO QUESTING FOR AND WITH GOD?

BRIAN'S PICTURE OF FAITH AS A QUEST HAS GOOD COMPANY. SOME OF THE MOST FAMOUS WRITINGS IN CHRISTIAN HISTORY FEATURE DRAMATIC JOURNEYS. DANTE'S *DIVINE COMEDY* AND JOHN BUNYAN'S *PILGRIM'S PROGRESS* ARE TWO CLASSICS.

Both Dante's *Divine Comedy* and Bunyan's *Pilgrim's Progress* can be accessed free of charge on the Gutenberg Project website. (Gutenberg.org)

EMBARKED.

GOD is THe WiND
iN THe saiL AND
THe sea we
saiL UPON; THe
SOURCe AND
GOAL OF OUR
Quest. HOW ARe
YOU EMBARKED
ON a journey
OF SeeKiNG GOD
AND KeePiNG THe
Quest aLiVe?

Brian's words steer us away
from passive, disinterested,
academic theorizing.
• If you "are embarked," what is at
stake in your quest for God?
• How important has your relationship
with God been to you?
• Are you comfortable with that level of
value? How would you work to change it?
• Sketch or describe your
thoughts in your Journal.

"THE GREAT FRENCH PHILOSOPHER BLAISE PASCAL
SAID IT SIMPLY AND WELL: 'WE ARE EMBARKED.' IN
OTHER WORDS, WE AREN'T JUST THEORIZING ABOUT A
HYPOTHETICAL JOURNEY OR PLANNING A POTENTIAL
VOYAGE FOR SOMEDAY IN THE FUTURE. WE ARE
ALREADY AT SEA, ACTUALLY UNDERWAY, IN A WILD
ADVENTURE OF SUN AND SEA AND TIDE."

Discuss Brian's question.
Then picture the blessed space
between. Work together to build a
devotional practice based on the quest
for life "in between the extremes." Plan the
way a person might come before God in
both an image-rich and a humble, image-
shedding practice. What habits of
devotion would help us steer between
the two rocks into that blessed
quest Brian describes?

Before close your first session together, ask questions about today's experience with
Animate. Build your next session based on group feedback. Remind the group to explore
their Journals in the time between now and your next session. What parts of the
Journal did you spend lots of time discussing? What parts were simply touched upon?
Encourage members to go deeper and share their findings the next time you gather.

RELIGION | SPIRITUALITY IS NOT ENOUGH
LILLIAN DANIEL

WHERE DO YOU GROW; WHERE DO YOU THRIVE?

Brian McLaren encouraged us to reflect on what it means to be embarked on a quest for God. In this session, Lillian Daniel helps us reclaim religion, saying that spirituality is not enough. Lillian encourages us to root ourselves in the depths of the Christian tradition—its history and texts, beliefs, and practices.

FILL YOUR MEETING SPACE with flowers—some cut and some rooted in pots. (Check first for any flower allergies). Play some music that might set a tongue-in-cheek tone such as "Give Me That Old Time Religion," "For All the Saints," or even, "In the Garden!"

Read through Lillian's bio together.
• What do you think of Lillian's views on faith?
• Have you ever found yourself stuck trying to figure out what it means to be a person of faith? How did you move past it?
• Do you tend to cling to church traditions or stray away from the church? What calls you to be a part of this group?

Lillian is impatient with people who call themselves spiritual but not religious because in her opinion, being spiritual is not enough. Take a look at her flower metaphor together. Invite the group to circle, color, highlight, and doodle with the words that stand out for them. Take some time to unpack this significant idea together.
• Have you ever considered yourself spiritual but not religious? Why or why not?
• How have you rooted yourself in faith or vice versa?
• Circle the stage of plant growth in the Journal where you see yourself in this moment. Or draw an alternative stage of your own.
• Would you say you are growing or wilting? Why?

Reclaiming Religion

FOR LILLIAN DANIEL, FAITH ISN'T SOMETHING WE MAKE FOR OURSELVES. IT'S A LONG, HARDY TRADITION THAT WE ENTER AND ADD TO. SHE PUSHES BACK AT THE IDEA THAT IT'S POSSIBLE TO BE "SPIRITUAL" WITHOUT BEING "RELIGIOUS."

FOR MANY PEOPLE TODAY, THIS QUESTION OF WHAT IT MEANS TO BE A PERSON OF FAITH HAS BECOME A STICKING POINT. IT KEEPS SOME PEOPLE AWAY FROM THE CHURCH. IT KEEPS OTHERS CLINGING TO TRADITIONS THAT MAY HAVE LOST THEIR MEANING. SO WHAT SHOULD WE MAKE OF THIS OFTEN MUDDY, WEEDY GARDEN OF RELIGION THAT WE FIND OURSELVES IN?

LILLIAN'S BOOKS:

• TELL IT LIKE IT IS: RECLAIMING THE PRACTICE OF TESTIMONY
• THIS ODD AND WONDROUS CALLING: THE PUBLIC AND PRIVATE LIVES OF TWO MINISTERS

MORE LILLIAN TRIVIA:

• SENIOR MINISTER OF FIRST CONGREGATIONAL CHURCH IN GLEN ELLYN, ILLINOIS
• CO-HOSTS A WEEKLY TV PROGRAM IN CHICAGO CALLED 30 GOOD MINUTES
• FREQUENT CONTRIBUTOR TO CHRISTIAN CENTURY MAGAZINE AND THE HUFFINGTON POST
• WON THE DISTINGUISHED ALUMNI AWARD AT YALE DIV. SCHOOL

• MDIV. FROM YALE UNIVERSITY DIVINITY SCHOOL

GREEN-GRO SEEDS

animate

IN 2011, LILLIAN WROTE AN ONLINE DEVOTIONAL CALLED, "SPIRITUAL BUT NOT RELIGIOUS: STOP BORING ME." THE PIECE WENT VIRAL. IT DREW STRONG AGREEMENT FROM SOME, VEHEMENT DISAGREEMENT FROM OTHERS. (HTTP://WWW.UCC.ORG/FEED-YOUR-SPIRIT/DAILY-DEVOTIONAL/SPIRITUAL-BUT-NOT-RELIGIOUS.HTML)

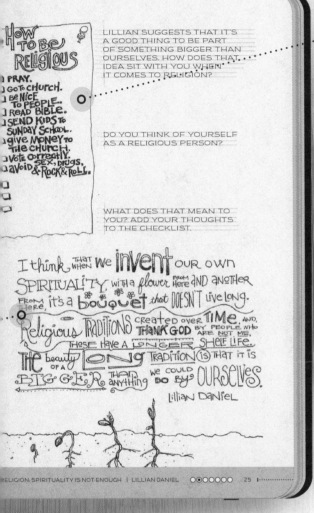

LILLIAN SUGGESTS THAT IT'S A GOOD THING TO BE PART OF SOMETHING BIGGER THAN OURSELVES. HOW DOES THAT IDEA SIT WITH YOU WHEN IT COMES TO RELIGION?

DO YOU THINK OF YOURSELF AS A RELIGIOUS PERSON?

WHAT DOES THAT MEAN TO YOU? ADD YOUR THOUGHTS TO THE CHECKLIST.

Take time to free-associate with the word "religion." Have someone record words people offer that describe religion. Invite people to offer their personal definitions of and experiences with religion. Work through the checklist and questions in the Journal together.
- If you do something "religiously," what does that mean to you?
- How do you think colloquial use of the word "religious" affects the meaning of being a religious Christian?
- Why do you consider yourself "religious" or "not religious"?
- What would you add to the checklist?

* CONSIDER THIS EXPANSION

to the group activity. Make a larger version of the checklist on a whiteboard or chart paper. See how many points the group can add. Coax them into honesty about this topic. Allow for snarky stereotypes to come out in addition to sincere thoughts. Invite them to study the group's list and then write down several of their favorites on sticky notes. Have them post their selections together as kind of a top-ten list on "How to be Religious."

LOOK UP THE DEFINITIONS

of "religion" and "spiritual" in a dictionary. Did you find what you expected? How do they relate to your personal definitions? Bring these thoughts to the discussion.

Want to dig deeper into the Latin roots of the word "religion"? Irmgard Busch, in her article "Religie," asserts that the word "religion" could be derived from either the verbs *religare* or *relegere. Religare* means to bind together or to connect, while *relegere* is the action of considering or examining something repeatedly, observing something over and over again. Busch writes: "Religion, therefore, is a factor that creates cohesion and solidarity within groups and societies." (Hedy d'Ancona et al., eds., *Vrouwenlexicon: Tweehonderd jaar emancipatie van A tot Z* (Utrecht: Het Spectrum, 1989), 324-5).

Watch the video together.
• What seems most important
about religion to Lillian?
• What would the kind of religion
Lillian's talking about look like?
• What would it look like to be
spiritual but not religious?
• What is it about organized religion
that turns people off?
• What makes being spiritual but
not religious attractive?

A 2009 *NEWSWEEK* POLL FOUND THAT 30% OF AMERICANS
ARE "SPIRITUAL BUT NOT RELIGIOUS," WHILE 48% ARE "BOTH
RELIGIOUS AND SPIRITUAL." (HTTP://WWW.THEDAILYBEAST.COM/
NEWSWEEK/2009/04/06/ONE-NATION-UNDER-GOD.HTML)

WHAT DOES IT MEAN TO BE SPIRITUAL? WHEN A 1999 GALLUP
SURVEY ASKED PEOPLE TO DEFINE "SPIRITUALITY," ALMOST A
THIRD DEFINED IT WITHOUT REFERENCE TO GOD OR A HIGHER
AUTHORITY: "A CALMNESS IN MY LIFE," "SOMETHING YOU
REALLY PUT YOUR HEART INTO," OR "LIVING THE LIFE YOU
FEEL IS PLEASING." ((HTTP://WWW.GALLUP.COM/POLL/7759/
AMERICANS-SPIRITUAL-SEARCHES-TURN-INWARD.ASPX)

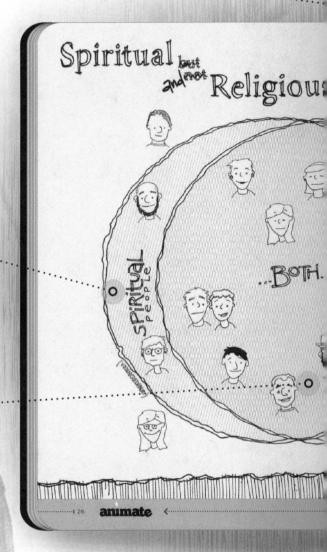

Invite group members to draw
where they really see themselves
within the Venn diagram in the Journal.
• Do you consider yourself religious but not
spiritual (what would that even look like?),
spiritual and religious, or spiritual but not
religious? Have an open conversation about where
members in your group see themselves and why.
• Where would you put Jesus in this diagram? After some
initial thoughts, divvy up the following passages from
the Gospel of Luke to deepen the group's conversation:
Luke 9:1-6; Luke 11:1-4; Luke 11:37-44; Luke 13:22-
30; Luke 14:1-6; Luke 17:11-19; Luke 18:9-17; Luke
21:1-6; Luke 24:13-35. Provide time for reading
and reflection, and then have group members
summarize their passage and indicate
where they think it situates
Jesus on the diagram.

RELIGION ·····> There is a Spiritual But Not Religious website at sbnr.org. The mission statement is: "SBNR.org serves the global population of
individuals who walk a spiritual path outside traditional religion. This is your home for open source spirituality." You can read more
about this topic in an article by Robert C. Fuller, a Religious Studies Prof. at Bradley University, called, "Spiritual but Not Religious,"
(http://www.beliefnet.com/Entertainment/Books/2002/07/Spiritual-But-Not-Religious.aspx)

HOW IS YOUR GROUP RESPONDING

to Lillian's video? She makes a strong argument against the individualization of religion. Does your group tend to agree or disagree? Make sure everyone feels welcome into the conversation—especially those who may feel like Lillian has criticized their point of view.

Divide your class into two groups. Assign one to be "Religious" and the other "Spiritual but Not Religious." Facilitate a lively debate between the two groups about which group is better. Afterward, talk about what's appealing about both sides of the argument.

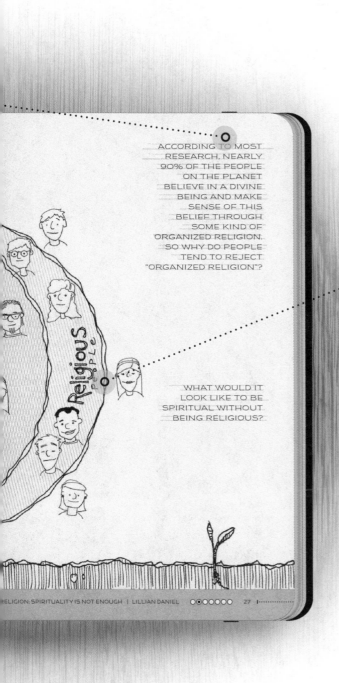

ACCORDING TO MOST RESEARCH, NEARLY 90% OF THE PEOPLE ON THE PLANET BELIEVE IN A DIVINE BEING AND MAKE SENSE OF THIS BELIEF THROUGH SOME KIND OF ORGANIZED RELIGION. SO WHY DO PEOPLE TEND TO REJECT "ORGANIZED RELIGION"?

WHAT WOULD IT LOOK LIKE TO BE SPIRITUAL WITHOUT BEING RELIGIOUS?

ReligiouS PEOPLE

RELIGION: SPIRITUALITY IS NOT ENOUGH | LILLIAN DANIEL ○○○○○○ 27

"ANYONE CAN FIND GOD ALONE ON A PICTURESQUE MOUNTAINTOP, THE HIKING TRAIL, OR THE SUNSET. THE MIRACLE IS THAT I CAN FIND GOD IN THE COMPANY OF OTHER PEOPLE WHO ARE JUST AS ANNOYING AS I AM." – LILLIAN DANIEL

AMONG CRITICS OF ORGANIZED RELIGION, THERE IS NONE MORE VEHEMENT THAN CHRISTOPHER HITCHENS. IN A 2007 TALK ON FREE SPEECH, HITCHENS CONTENDED THAT ORGANIZED RELIGION IS "THE MAIN SOURCE OF HATRED IN THE WORLD." HE ADDED, "I THINK [RELIGION] SHOULD BE . . . TREATED WITH RIDICULE AND HATRED AND CONTEMPT." (HTTP://WWW. YOUTUBE.COM/WATCH?V=Y30TS5GSOOE‡FEATURE=RELMFU)

Christopher Hitchens's most organized case against religion is his book, *God Is Not Great: How Religion Poisons Everything* (New York: Hachette Book Group, 2007).

Read the quote in the middle of the page together. Hebrews 12:1-2 pictures the "great cloud of witnesses" — faithful folk whose faithful example supports us in our journey. Invite group members to share about someone who has influenced and inspired their faith. Some will be famous saints (Mother Teresa, MLK, St. Francis, et al.), but some will be everyday people. Have them add those people to the trellis. Then talk about the questions in the Journal together.

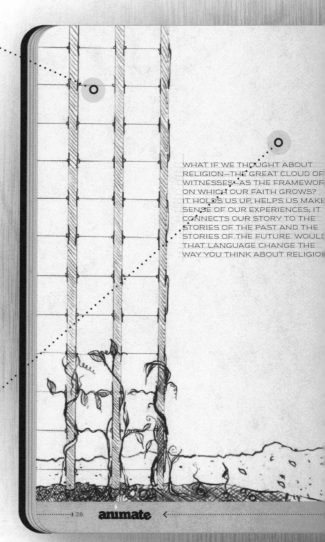

WHAT IF WE THOUGHT ABOUT RELIGION—THE GREAT CLOUD OF WITNESSES—AS THE FRAMEWORK ON WHICH OUR FAITH GROWS? IT HOLDS US UP, HELPS US MAKE SENSE OF OUR EXPERIENCES; IT CONNECTS OUR STORY TO THE STORIES OF THE PAST AND THE STORIES OF THE FUTURE. WOULD THAT LANGUAGE CHANGE THE WAY YOU THINK ABOUT RELIGION?

"I FINALLY FOUND SOME AMAZING [CHURCHES] THAT I COULD CALL HOME. AND THOSE PLACES DIDN'T JUST MEET MY NEEDS. I LIKE TO THINK THAT THEY CHANGED MY NEEDS—THAT THESE COMMUNITIES OF FAITH SHAPED ME AND CHALLENGED ME AND HELPED ME TO GROW CLOSER TO GOD."

If you are meeting in a church building, consider walking the hallways and sanctuary, noticing portraits on the walls, considering the people who have come before in that community, actually imagining "the great cloud of witnesses" in that church. If you are not meeting in a church, do the imaginative journey together, considering those who have gone before and what they've contributed to the faith life of your community. Do their voices affirm religious adherence, spiritual enrichment, both?

* HAVE THE GROUP REVISIT

the plant growth stages at the bottom of this spread. Unpack the imagery: what's the soil, the trellis, the seed? Who or what is needed for growth? What's missing? Invite them to draw what they envision to be their next stage of faith development. Do they see their growth happening with or without the support of the trellis?

Marry a Pregnant Virgin: Unusual Bible Stories for New and Curious Christians by Frank G. Honeycutt (Augsburg Books, 2008) is a great introduction to the Bible's inspirational stories of people's faith and life in God.

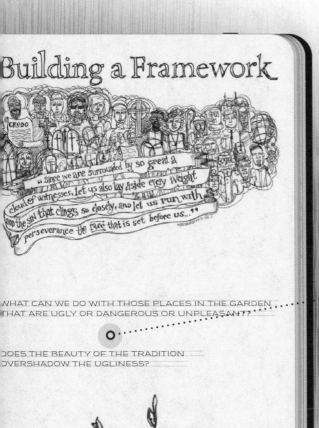

Building a Framework

" Since we are surrounded by so great a cloud of witnesses, let us also lay aside every weight and the sin that clings so closely, and let us run with perseverance the race that is set before us... "

HEBREWS 12:1

WHAT CAN WE DO WITH THOSE PLACES IN THE GARDEN THAT ARE UGLY OR DANGEROUS OR UNPLEASANT?

○

DOES THE BEAUTY OF THE TRADITION OVERSHADOW THE UGLINESS?

RELIGION: SPIRITUALITY IS NOT ENOUGH | LILLIAN DANIEL   ○●○○○○○   29

"IT'S PRETTY EASY TO PLAY BY THE RULES OF A RELIGION IN WHICH YOU WRITE YOUR OWN SCRIPT. MUCH HARDER TO FIND MEANING IN THE WORDS OF A BOOK THAT WE DID NOT WRITE FOR OURSELVES, FROM A VERY DIFFERENT TIME." – LILLIAN DANIEL

Lillian reminds us that the Bible pushes Christians out of narcissistic self-interest. Open Bibles in your group to Matthew 5:21-48 and read the "antitheses," the places where Jesus challenges us to go beyond normal expectations.
• What are the challenges in these verses?
• What impact does Jesus' high demand have on you?
• What impact has Jesus' high demand had on the world?
• How would your religious practices change if they were built on these words?

JESUS ONCE SAID, "ANYONE WHO DOES THE WILL OF MY FATHER IS MY MOTHER OR BROTHER OR SISTER." (MARK 3:31-35) MAYBE THAT'S WHY THE EARLIEST CHRISTIANS CALLED ONE ANOTHER "BROTHER" AND "SISTER." THEY RELIED ON ONE ANOTHER AS COMMUNITY BECAUSE BY BECOMING CHRISTIANS MANY EXPERIENCED THE REJECTION OF THEIR FAMILIES.

"TIRED OF DECORATING OUR LIVES WITH BOUQUETS
OF OUR OWN CHOOSING, WE'RE READY TO GO DEEPER,
AND EVEN READY TO PUT IN THE WORK IT REQUIRES.
BECAUSE BEING PART OF A RELIGIOUS TRADITION
TAKES WORK." – LILLIAN DANIEL

Some of the flowers pictured
in the Journal have deep roots in the
earth. Others are attached to chopsticks,
like Lillian's mother's flowers. Invite the group
to write in some parts of their personal religion
that they feel are deeply rooted and some that
may seem beautiful but might not be as strong.
• What did you discover as you reflected
on your own religious experience?
• How have you put work into your
religious beliefs and practices?
• What have you maybe glossed over or spent less
time with that you might focus on in the future?
• If you disagree with Lillian, how might you be able
to develop a religion "of [y]our own choosing"
that is challenging and meaningful?

ON MANY OCCASIONS THE NEW TESTAMENT
DESCRIBES "STAGES" OF CHRISTIAN GROWTH;
FOR EXAMPLE, IN JAMES 1:19-27, GALATIANS
5:13-25; 2 PETER 1:3-8, AND ROMANS 12.

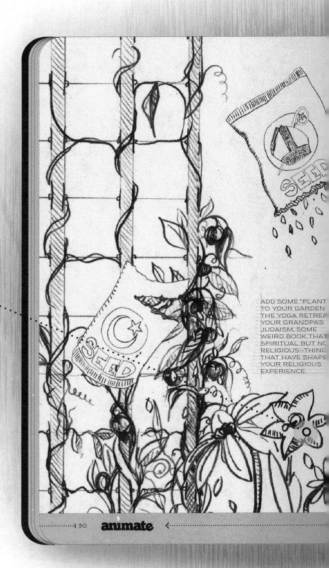

ADD SOME "PLANT[...]
TO YOUR GARDEN[...]
THE YOGA RETREA[...]
YOUR GRANDPA'S
JUDAISM, SOME
WEIRD BOOK THA[...]
SPIRITUAL BUT N[...]
RELIGIOUS—THING[...]
THAT HAVE SHAPE[...]
YOUR RELIGIOUS
EXPERIENCE.

animate

GROUPS WILL VARY WIDELY ON THIS TOPIC.

Be prepared to listen well so that you can animate the conversation
in helpful ways. If you have many who are born-and-bred traditional
Christians, the conversation will look much different than if your group is
made up of people who have recently found their way to a church group.

HOW WELL DO YOU KNOW YOUR OWN

tradition? Facilitating this conversation may require some research on your part. What are the valuable fruits and blossoms of your own tradition that could be lifted up for the group? Denominational web sites are a great places to learn what your tradition believes and how it lives out faith today.

Seeding the Soil

WHAT'S BEEN VALUABLE IN YOUR TRADITION?

WHAT HAVE YOU GATHERED FROM OTHER TRADITIONS THAT HAVE MADE YOUR FAITH MORE MEANINGFUL?

RELIGION: SPIRITUALITY IS NOT ENOUGH I LILLIAN DANIEL ⦾◯◯◯◯◯◯ 31 I. . . . .

One appeal of personal spirituality is the prospect of collecting from various religions. Invite group members to use smartphones or other devices to find some practices from other religions that appeal to them—Islam, Judaism, Buddhism, etc. Have them write the practices they notice in their Journals.
• What practices from other religions appeal to you and why?
• What have you gathered from other traditions that have made your faith more meaningful?
• Why do you think some people are resistant to incorporating practices from other religions?

SAINT AUGUSTINE WAS GLAD TO BORROW CONCEPTS FROM PAGAN CULTURE IN ORDER TO BETTER UNDERSTAND GOD AND THE GOSPEL. HE CALLED THE GEMS OF PLATONISM "EGYPT'S GOLD," REFERRING TO THE WAY ISRAEL ESCAPED EGYPT WITH GOLD PLUNDERED FROM THEIR CAPTORS.

THE "HISTORY OF RELIGIONS" SCHOOL OF THE NINETEENTH CENTURY WAS AN APPROACH TO CHRISTIANITY THAT TRACED ITS BASIC BELIEFS AND RITUALS TO PAGAN RELIGIOUS TRADITIONS FROM THE SURROUNDING CULTURES. FOR EXAMPLE, BAPTISM AS A RITUAL OF DYING AND RISING HAS PARALLELS IN THE RITUALS OF ANCIENT MITHRAISM. SOME CHRISTIANS FEEL THREATENED BY THIS IDEA THAT THEIR FAITH MAY HAVE SIMILARITIES TO OTHER BELIEF SYSTEMS, OTHERS SEE THIS EVIDENCE OF GOD'S MORE INCLUSIVE LOVE FOR THE WORLD.

Saint Augustine was a fourth-century saint from North Africa. His allusion to the value of Plato's philosophy as a framework for Christian doctrine is from On Christian Doctrine 40.60.

Lillian found her own flourish by tapping into the time-honored tradition of Christianity.
• What are the advantages of having a long history of faith?
• What advantage might come from having ancestors in faith who lived 2,000 years ago? What challenges does that present?
• Have you found a place in a garden bigger than your own?
• What would draw you to place deeper roots in the Christian religious tradition?

JESUS' FAMOUS "PARABLE OF THE SOWER"
and other Kingdom parables in Matthew 13:1-43 could offer some great support to any conversation about putting down roots.

Hosea 14 is a call for people to return to God. Read this beautiful passage of fresh blooming together. What's surprisingly absent in many conversations about the relative value of spirituality versus religion is, ironically, God!
• Where is God in Hosea 14?
• What's God doing?
• What are the qualities of God?
• What insights does this text offer related to God's role in our "blooming" today?

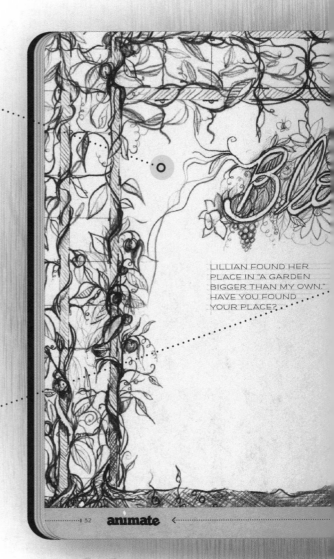

LILLIAN FOUND HER PLACE IN "A GARDEN BIGGER THAN MY OWN." HAVE YOU FOUND YOUR PLACE?

animate

"THE BEAUTY OF A LONG TRADITION IS THAT IT IS BIGGER THAN ANYTHING WE COULD DO BY OURSELVES. THESE DAYS IT IS SOMEWHAT COUNTERCULTURAL TO SUGGEST THAT ONE MIGHT POSSIBLY BENEFIT FROM THE COMPANY OF OTHERS IN THE LIFE OF FAITH. PARTICULARLY THOSE WHO HAVE GONE BEFORE US IN FAITH ... I WANTED MORE THAN JUST AN INTELLECTUAL EPIPHANY ... SOMETHING WITH A LONGER SHELF LIFE THAN MY OWN LATEST OPINION." – LILLIAN DANIEL

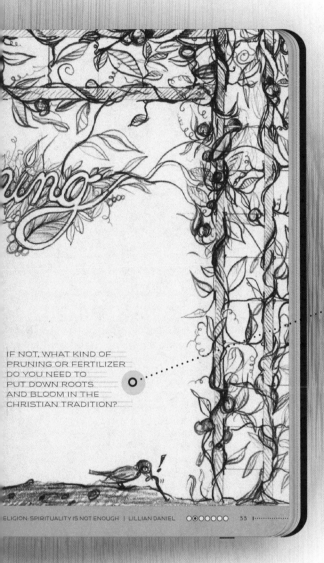

IF NOT, WHAT KIND OF
PRUNING OR FERTILIZER
DO YOU NEED TO
PUT DOWN ROOTS
AND BLOOM IN THE
CHRISTIAN TRADITION?

THE PHILOSOPHER GEORGE SANTAYANA FAMOUSLY SAID, "THOSE WHO CANNOT REMEMBER THE PAST ARE DOOMED TO REPEAT IT." (LIFE OF REASON I) PARAPHRASE: WE LEARN HISTORY IN ORDER TO AVOID ITS MISTAKES. WHEN YOU THINK ABOUT IT, THAT IS A VERY NEGATIVE VIEW OF HISTORY. HOW OFTEN DOES AN EMPHASIS ON PAST MISTAKES KEEP US FROM SEEING THE VALUE OF ORGANIZED RELIGION?

Look up 1 Corinthians 12:12-26 and Romans 12:3-8.
• How does Paul picture the church?
• What part of the "body of Christ" are you?
• In the Journal, list three unique gifts you bring to the group.
• How could we use all of our gifts to create a strong religious community?
• How much more challenging would it be to create a community on your own with only your gifts?

Animated conversations bubble over, so don't be surprised if you've lost track of time. How will you extend your conversation between sessions? Consider assigning research projects, creating social media pages, or identifying ways your group can help each other bloom and bear fruit for God in that space between the spiritual and the religious.

JESUS | THE REVOLUTION OF LOVE
MARK SCANDRETTE

WHAT MIGHT YOU NEED TO RISK IN ORDER TO
LIVE MORE FULLY IN THE REVOLUTION OF LOVE?

In the last session, Lillian asserted her belief that spirituality is not enough. In this session, Mark guides us to think differently about living in Jesus' way. It began with a moment of truth: Mark realized that his sermons weren't doing anything important. What to do?!!? He decided to make church a place of practice rather than just belief and learning. The rest is history.

HOW WILL YOU WELCOME YOUR GROUP?

Consider the architectural transition of the Journal throughout this session—from Gothic church to Dojo. How might that affect the way you set the room? Consider playing some music as people arrive, such as "Revolution" by the Beatles, anticipating Mark's "Revolution of Love."

Here's how the ReImagine website describes their ministry: "As a community we emphasize and pursue orthopraxis, a congruency of right belief and right living—resonating with the Apostle who said, 'Watch your life and doctrine closely, persevere in them.' (I Timothy 4:16). We recognize that how we live is equally important to what we say we believe." Have your group open to 1 Timothy 4:4-16. Talk about how this text suggests action on behalf of the reader.
• What belief is most important to your faith?
• What actions does that belief suggest?

Mark talks about Jesus in a way that may be new to your group. He turns inactive, passive learning into active doing in the world. This kind of discipleship might be surprising for some people.. Talk about your group's perceptions of Jesus. How might a Jesus enshrined in stone cathedrals differ from the Jesus of the Gospels?

"THE KIND OF LIFE THAT JESUS LIVED AND INVITES US INTO IS IMPOSSIBLE. AND MAYBE IT IS, APART FROM A SOURCE OF LOVE AND POWER THAT'S GREATER THAN OUR OWN. BUT THE ONLY WAY WE'RE GOING TO DISCOVER THAT LOVE AND POWER IS BY TAKING THE RISK TO TRY AND LIVE INTO THE IMPOSSIBILITY OF THE GOSPEL."
—MARK SCANDRETTE

JESUS: ➤ Check out Mark's community at reimagine.org.

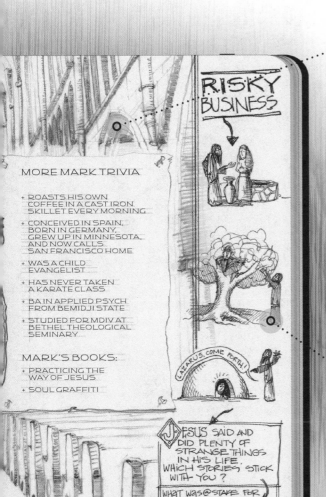

MORE MARK TRIVIA

+ ROASTS HIS OWN COFFEE IN A CAST IRON SKILLET EVERY MORNING
+ CONCEIVED IN SPAIN, BORN IN GERMANY, GREW UP IN MINNESOTA, AND NOW CALLS SAN FRANCISCO HOME
+ WAS A CHILD EVANGELIST
+ HAS NEVER TAKEN A KARATE CLASS
+ BA IN APPLIED PSYCH FROM BEMIDJI STATE
+ STUDIED FOR MDIV AT BETHEL THEOLOGICAL SEMINARY

MARK'S BOOKS:

+ PRACTICING THE WAY OF JESUS
+ SOUL GRAFFITI

RISKY BUSINESS

LAZARUS, COME FORTH!

JESUS SAID AND DID PLENTY OF STRANGE THINGS IN HIS LIFE. WHICH STORIES STICK WITH YOU?

WHAT WAS @ STAKE FOR JESUS WHEN HE DID THOSE THINGS?

ESUS: THE REVOLUTION OF LOVE | MARK SCANDRETTE ○○○○○○○ 4i |

Soren Kierkegaard once sat in the state church in Copenhagen. The Bible was gilded. The sanctuary had silk and velvet appointments and ornate stained glass. Someone read scripture quoting God, "I do not dwell in temples made with hands." Kierkegaard responded by saying, "I looked around, and no one was laughing!" Talk together about these types of experiences. Sketch yourselves into the pews and ponder whether you have ever had one of those moments when the raw truth of scripture or Christian truth suddenly struck you as incongruous with the reality of church.

* OUR TOPIC IS JESUS, THE MASTER,

the center of Christian passion and for some, a very emotional subject. Take time to know your emotions and convictions concerning Jesus before you welcome your group. Remember your role: animate the conversation!

Jesus turned many cultural norms upside down and provided new and unexpected ways of thinking about things. This was a risky venture, and it made the rulers of the day feel like their power was being threatened. Form three groups based on the story sketches in the Journal: Woman at the Well (John 4), Zacchaeus (Luke 19), and Lazarus (John 11). Ask each group to create a contemporary version of their story as a skit or sketch. Talk about how these stories relate to society today.
• Who is a modern example of each character in these stories?
• How might Jesus respond to each if he were around today?
• Read John 17:14-18. When does being a Christ follower feel like risky business?

Soren Kierkegaard (1813-1855), a Danish philosopher and a passionate Christian, developed existentialism. He critiqued the church in his time for its staid and hyper-rational ways. Kierkegaard pictured a riskier Christianity, one that didn't need full rational proof before it took action. He called that risk a "leap of faith."

WHERE ARE PEOPLE AT WITH JESUS?

Before you watch the video, invite your group to share from memory some of their favorite scenes from the Gospels. Then have the group free associate verbs that describe the actions of Jesus. Have one member record the verbs on a whiteboard or chart paper. Throughout this session, center your energies on doing!

Watch the video together.
Have someone write the verbs and scenes Mark features on the same white board or chart paper you used before the video. Compare your group's ideas and views with Mark's. He and his church try to read the Bible to find not only what Jesus people *believe*, but especially what Jesus people *practice*. Mark and his community did some unexpected and unusual things, like selling half their possessions and sharing private failings with one another.
• What unusual or unexpected things did Jesus do?
• What unusual things does Jesus inspire you to do?

Mark encourages us to think outside the church. His image of the Jesus Dojo puts Christianity into a fully active environment. You don't just sit and learn in a dojo; you do.
• When you are in worship, what do you feel drawn to? Spending more time in worship in a sanctuary? Going out into the world? Just going home? Why is that?
• Do you ever feel like churches are boxes that confine Jesus? Why or why not?
• How can you morph a church building into a place that "does," not just a place that "is"?
• How does Mark's concept of the Jesus Dojo interact with this idea?

THE FIRST "CHURCH" BUILDINGS WERE BUILT AFTER CONSTANTINE MADE CHRISTIANITY THE OFFICIAL RELIGION OF ROME IN 311 C.E. BEFORE THAT, BEING CHRISTIAN COULD BE DANGEROUS. A CHURCH BUILDING WOULD HAVE BEEN LIKE A BIG TARGET, SO CHRISTIANS MET IN PRIVATE HOMES.

L. Michael White, *Building God's House in the Roman World*, (Baltimore: Md.: Johns Hopkins University Press, 1990).

For more, check out these resources.
Mark Scandrette, *Practicing the Way of Jesus*, (Nottingham, U.K.: Inter-Varsity Press, 2011).
Dallas Willard, *The Divine Conspiracy*, (New York: HarperOne, 1998).
Eric Mataxas, *Bonhoeffer: Pastor, Martyr, Prophet, Spy*, (Nashville, Tenn.: Thomas Nelson, 2011).

JESUS: THE REVOLUTION OF LOVE | MARK SCANDRETTE ○○○○○○ 43

Have your group look over these three contrasting versions of Jesus ministry—the authentic one on the right versus our modern permutations to the left. What happened between then and now? Do the original accounts offer anything to help us reclaim the way of Jesus? Divide up the group to read Luke 5:1-11, John 13:1-17, and John 4. Invite the group to replace or modify the "ideas" to the left with a modern practice that's more consistent with walking in Jesus' way.

Dietrich Bonhoeffer required his seminary students to meditate on each day's Bible passage long enough to discern what God wanted them to do. Give this a try in your group. Have everyone chose one of the scenes from the Gospels depicted in the first two spreads of this session. Have them find and silently read their passage. Keep the focus on what we could DO, not what we think or believe. Simply, what does this part of the Jesus story prompt me to DO? Try to gracefully push your group past the hypothetical into actual and accountable practices. Allow time for people to share.

* NOTICE HOW CATHEDRAL IS BEGINNING to morph into dojo on this page? In 1896 the architect Louis Sullivan said, "form follows function." Check out the directions for renovation in the Journal. How would your group further the transformation? Invite them to sketch or note their thoughts.

Dietrich Bonhoeffer resisted Adolf Hitler's Nazism. He wrote, preached, and taught Christian resistance to the evil of his time. His underground seminary trained leaders of this resistance. He was executed by the Nazis a few days before the end of World War II.

THE JOURNAL HELPS US ASK, "WHO IS JESUS?"

This is both a question of truth and a personal question we need to ask ourselves. Who is Jesus? And who is Jesus to me? Mark wants to move us from belief into practice, but he does not want us to stop believing or talking about belief. So here's the time to ask who Jesus is.

Read through the five visions of Jesus in the Journal together. Give group members time to rate or give weight to the views of Jesus they most relate to in the Journal. The Confession of Chalcedon (451) calls Jesus "perfect in Godhead and also perfect in manhood; truly God and truly man, of a reasonable [rational] soul and body."

• Why does it matter how we define the divinity and humanity of Jesus?

• Discuss the problem of a merely human Jesus, stuck in the bookstore next to all the other wise self-help gurus.

• Discuss the place of the only divine Jesus, walking a foot above ground—much too far from the daily issues of living that you and I face.

 THE QUESTION ANSWERED AT CHALCEDON WAS NOT INVENTED IN THE FIFTH CENTURY. THE CONVERSATION BEGAN WITH FIRST-CENTURY BIBLICAL PICTURES OF JESUS' DIVINITY LIKE JOHN 1:1-5, 14, 18; HEBREWS 1:1-4; AND PHILIPPIANS 2:6-11.

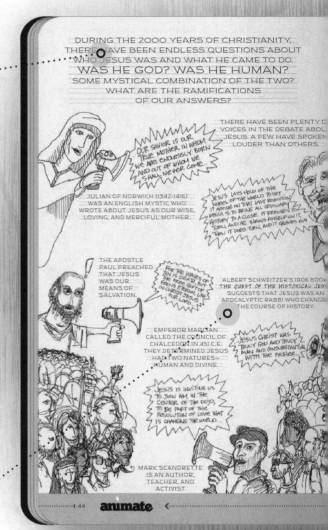

CONVERSATION ABOUT THESE FIVE

different views of Jesus might seem to make Jesus into an inkblot whose identity is completely dependent on the eye of the beholder. Listen for that in your group. Be ready to talk about the parameters that the Gospels set for understanding who Jesus is. For example, Jesus as military conqueror (as in Constantine and the Crusades) doesn't work well with Mark 8:31ff., where Jesus insists that he was sent not to conquer but to die.

 "INSTEAD OF BRINGING IN THE ESCHATOLOGICAL CONDITIONS, JESUS HAS DESTROYED THEM. THE WHEEL ROLLS ONWARD, AND THE MANGLED BODY OF THE ONE IMMEASURABLY GREAT MAN . . . IS HANGING UPON IT STILL. THAT IS HIS VICTORY AND HIS REIGN." –ALBERT SCHWEITZER

If you want more views of Jesus to talk about, St. Francis painted a picture of Jesus as Pauper. She said, "I married Lady Poverty, widowed since Christ." Or you could see Jesus as Macho Man in books like *No More Mr. Christian Nice Guy* and *The Church Impotent—the Feminization of Christianity*. These authors picture Jesus as very macho with big biceps and tattoos.

Have group members flip through the Gospels to find three pieces of evidence that Jesus was divine and three pieces of evidence that Jesus was human. Allow some time for people to share what they found. Then look up Mark 15:40. In this verse, a Roman soldier at the cross watches Jesus breathe his last breath and says, "Surely this man was the Son of God."
• How can suffering and divinity coexist in Jesus?
• How would Jesus' experience have been different if he was wholly divine? What about if he was wholly human?
• Who is Jesus to YOU? Add your own face and one sentence expression of faith to your Journal.

Beginning in the first century, Christians identified some beliefs as outside the circle. These were later named "heresy." The letter we call 2 John warns about "those who don't believe Jesus came in the flesh." Some people think the writer is responding to an early version of "Docetism," the belief that Jesus only appeared to be fully human, but was really more of a spirit. Through the centuries, the church has often drawn lines like this.
• Add some bullet points to the "JESUS" list of things you know or believe about Jesus.
• Are there any views of Jesus that you consider to be "heresy"? Why or why not?
• How might your personal views of Jesus be considered "heretical" by other people?
• Jesus' ministry was all about crossing boundaries. What boundaries is Jesus calling you to cross? What does that say about who Jesus is to you?

For more information, check out Jaroslav Pelikan, *Jesus through the Centuries: His Place in the History of Culture.*

"IF I WAS GOING TO BE PART OF THIS REVOLUTION OF LOVE THAT JESUS EMBODIED AND PROMISED, I WOULD NEED TO BE MORE HONEST, MORE ACTIVE, AND MORE CONNECTED TO OTHER PEOPLE." —MARK SCANDRETTE

YOU HAVE ASKED ABOUT

Jesus' identity and puzzled over the tension between his divinity and humanity. Now you can help the group make a transition into daily life. What impact does what we know about Jesus have on who we are and what we do in the world? This transition from theory to practice fits perfectly with Mark's emphasis on *orthopraxis*—right doing.

Give the group some scriptural groceries to take with them this week as they continue to digest Mark's ideas and their own ideas about Jesus. Ground the actions in the scriptures that give rise to them. Encourage group members to write these scriptures in their Journals to read as they work through this spread this week.
Forgive—Matthew 18:21-35
(The Parable of the Unforgiving Servant)
Enemies—Matthew 5:43-48
(The Sermon on the Mount)
Wounded—Luke 10:25-37
(The Parable of the Good Samaritan)
Sick and in Prison—Matthew 25:31-40
(The Parable of the Sheep and the Goats)

Choose a couple of questions below to talk about in the group. Then encourage the group to think about the others throughout the week.
• What will fuel your Jesus actions?
• What does the divine-human Jesus have to do with the problems you face and the problems in your community?
• What about who Jesus was and the message he shared gives you hope that good intentions won't wilt in the light of day?
• Where would Jesus go first if he landed in your community today? Where do you think he's calling you to go?

BELIEFS FUEL ACTIONS. NEW YORK TIMES OP-ED COLUMNIST NICHOLAS KRISTOF REFLECTED ON HIS TRAVELS TO IMPOVERISHED AND SUFFERING POPULATIONS AROUND THE WORLD INCLUDING AIDS PATIENTS IN AFRICA, TSUNAMI VICTIMS IN JAPAN, AND SEX SLAVES IN SOUTHEAST ASIA. HE SUMMED UP WHAT HE SAW, SAYING, "THE RELIGIOUS PEOPLE STAY AND HELP LONGER." KRISTOF IS RIGHT. WHY? BECAUSE ONCE THE IMMEDIATE EMERGENCY RESPONSE AND THE RUSH OF NEWS COVERAGE FADE, "STAYING LONGER" REQUIRES A CONVICTION ABOUT THE PURPOSE OF OUR LIVES, ABOUT HOW GOD LOVES THE PEOPLE SERVED.

IN WHAT WAYS ARE FEEDING THE POOR, OR CARING FOR THE STRANGER REVOLUTIONARY ACTS?

WHAT'S YOUR MOTIVATION?

WE DON'T ALWAYS RECOGNIZE HOW RADICAL AND RISKY IT WAS FOR JESUS TO TALK TO WOMEN OR TOUCH LEPERS OR BREAK THE RELIGIOUS TRADITIONS OF HIS DAY. WHAT DO YOU THINK JESUS WAS UP TO WITH ALL OF THIS?

Read together John 9. This is by far the longest account of any of Jesus' healings. All the way through this chapter people are being challenged by Jesus' revolutionary love. Jesus takes calculated risks along the way, beginning with a course of treatment that breaks a number of Sabbath laws (9:5-7)!
• Of all the characters, who do you most relate to?
• What do you think was Jesus' motivation in healing this blind man?
• What would be the most challenging part of living in the way of Jesus?
• In what ways are healing the sick and feeding the poor revolutionary acts?

PREPARE YOUR PEOPLE TO GO

beyond good intentions. Help them make a plan to go humbly to the people they list and seek reconciliation. Encourage them to read around in the Gospels and actually imagine that the picture of Jesus should be imprinted in THEIR lives.

Healthy motivations matter to God. While the church is commonly thought to be expert at motivating through guilt and threat of punishment, this is not the way of Jesus. Passages like John 13:34-35 and John 14:15-17 speak to the motivation of love and the empowerment of the Holy Spirit.

43

THIS IS WHERE YOU IMAGINE WITH YOUR GROUP

what their week looks like in light of the Jesus Dojo/Revolution of Love. How will they continue the good that God has been doing in and among them beyond your time together? Finish where Mark finishes, asking his pointed questions. Prepare the group to take one more step from the classroom into an active, Jesus-centered life.

Mark didn't go on this journey by himself. He got together with friends and with other faithful people to turn his life into a Revolution of Love. Work together through the following questions Mark asks at the end of the video and encourage your group to continue doing so beyond their time in the classroom.

Ask: Who can you get in the dojo to take those new risks with? Journal a list of people you want to have as practice partners. Emphasize that this is not an academic exercise. There's a big difference between talking about doing the Jesus thing and actually giving ourselves over to Master Jesus in the Dojo. This is the beginning of a commitment to practice what Master Jesus teaches.

Ask: Where do you most long for change in your life or healing for our world? Prayer and discernment do not usually resolve themselves in 30-second intervals. Prepare your group to be patient and to look long enough at their lives and the world to really hear their own heart beating in the "unforced rhythms of grace."

Ask: What might you need to risk in order to live more fully in the Revolution of Love that Jesus promised? Jesus told a parable about a man who built half a building and then ran out of money. Counting the cost is crucial to the realistic step from theory to practice. Calculate the risk. Identify the entanglements. Ask if they're ready to risk it. Have them journal these important steps.

animate

"THE PROMISE OF THE GOSPEL IS THAT WE CAN LEARN A WHOLE NEW WAY TO BE HUMAN, TO LIVE WITHOUT WORRY, FEAR, GREED, LUST, OR ANGER—TO LIVE A LIFE ANIMATED AND EMPOWERED BY LOVE."
—MARK SCANDRETTE

Re-create the conversation among Mark's friends that he mentions having after his Jesus Dojo epiphany. Talk about how your faith community could join in on Jesus' Revolution of Love. Whether in the closing moments of this session or between sessions, agree to hold one another accountable to one group or individual practice in the way of Jesus.

* BRAINSTORMING CONVERSATIONS like this one have the ability to change how people think about things. Keep in mind those people who might think this activity is just filler and find ways to invite them into the conversation in meaningful ways. Inspire participants to commit to this idea.

Mark's animating questions are huge. They are life changing. All conversation about practicing what we believe is ongoing. We are people in progress, so encourage continued dialog with the Journal and one another between sessions. But be sure to press your group past the talking into the doing. As they continue to live in Jesus' Revolution of Love, they can begin to wonder about the abundant life of salvation they'll hear about in the next session.

SALVATION | ABUNDANT LIFE NOW
SHANE HIPPS

ARE WE WILLING TO WAKE UP TO THE POSSIBILITY THAT THE
25550 DAYS WE HAVE ARE ACTUALLY THE MAIN COURSE?

Mark Scandrette brought us into the Jesus Dojo to explore the Jesus way. Today, Shane Hipps offers us images of salvation as we think about what happens during and after this life on earth. Shane invites us to consider the fundamental questions surrounding this "strange, beautiful, mysterious thing called existence."

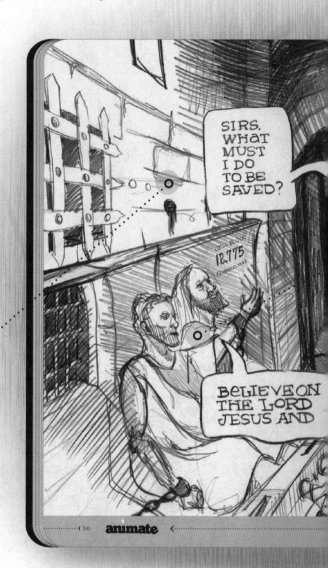

SET THE ROOM IN A "TIME-LY" FASHION.
Decorate with a variety of clocks, watches, and hourglasses all over the place. Consider playing music in the background such as "Does Anybody Really Know What Time It Is?" by Chicago, "Salvation is Here" by Lincoln Brewster, or the old gospel hymn "When the Role is Called Up Yonder."

START A VISIBLE STOPWATCH
in the room when you begin the session and let it run the whole time. See if anyone remembers to mention or notice it during class. You may have also noticed that each spread has an "Easter egg," a number that counts toward Shane's 25,550. The clock is ticking even as you meet.

Look at the Journal together. Give group members a chance to share a time when they've heard or experienced a conversation like this one. Some Christians believe they know the exact path to salvation. Others aren't so sure. Talk together about your group's ideas about salvation. Bring some ideas to share that your group might not have heard before.
- When have you heard the word "salvation"?
- What does salvation mean in your life?
- What ideas about salvation are you sure about? Unsure about?

THE WORD "SALVATION" APPEARS BETWEEN 120 AND 180 TIMES IN THE ENGLISH BIBLE, DEPENDING ON WHICH VERSION YOU READ. IN THE NRSV, "SALVATION" OCCURS 124 TIMES. IN THE ESV, IT APPEARS 178 TIMES.

Tell the story of Paul and Silas in prison from Acts 16.16-40; then have another person read Acts 16:28-31 aloud.
• What is the jailor asking for?
• When will he get it?
• Will it matter when he wakes up the next morning? Why or why not?
• Does the "household" get a choice in the matter? Why or why not?

ANCIENT PRISONS WERE HELLHOLES. THEY WERE VERY CROWDED. USUALLY, THEY WERE LOCATED BENEATH GROUND LEVEL AND DIDN'T HAVE ANY LIGHT. PRISONERS WERE GIVEN VERY LITTLE, VERY POOR FOOD AND WERE SURROUNDED BY DISEASE. SUICIDE RATES WERE HIGH. IT'S TOUGH TO IMAGINE A WHOLE LOT OF SINGING DOWN THERE, BUT PAUL AND SILAS SANG!

Salvation isn't easily definable. It's not something you can see, touch, or feel. In fact, it's even difficult to explain. Shane gives us some salvation images to consider. Give your group some time to sketch or write about some salvation images or experiences in their Journals. Then engage the questions:
• How would you describe the moments of salvation in your life?
• What do those moments suggest about what you believe it means or, even, doesn't mean to "be saved?"

THE HEBREW AND GREEK WORDS THAT ARE TRANSLATED INTO ENGLISH AS "SALVATION" OFTEN MEAN RESCUE FROM SOME KIND OF PERIL. SEE BIBLESTUDYTOOLS.COM AND OTHER ONLINE CONCORDANCES AND LEXICONS FOR MORE INFORMATION.

Craig Wansink's book, *Chained in Christ*, paints a vivid picture of ancient prisons and then explores the Apostle Paul's words about his times in prison.

SPEND SOME TIME WITH SHANE.

His own story is wider than the testimony he gives here about his knot and his dad's prayer. And messengers matter for our hearing of messages. How does Shane fit into the group's stereotypical image of evangelist or "salvation guy?"

Watch the video together.
But before you do, introduce the video with a quote from Shane: "Why am I here? What is the meaning of my life? Is this all there is? What happens when it's over? It's the thing that makes us different from the dolphins and donkeys, we are actually conscious of the fact that we are alive and one day, we know we will return to the dust." Start another stopwatch when it begins. Be ready to stop it when Shane finishes.
- How does Shane picture salvation?
- When does Shane see salvation happening?
- How do Shane's ideas about salvation interplay with your own beliefs?
- Is all of this what the Philippian jailer was seeking? Is it what you and people you love seek? Why or why not?

SHANE'S EMPHASIS ON SALVATION

as present tense reality may be new to some of your people. In fact, it may be distressing! Be ready for and welcome distress and dissent. Guide the conversation in a healthy direction by asking people to share their own thoughts and opinions and by keeping an open table for all ideas.

It's time to offer some reflection time for your group members. You and each person in the room have personal reasons for being a part of a small group. Perhaps some of these reasons have to do with salvation, perhaps not. Point out that Shane used to pitch Guinness and Porsche as a marketing guy.
- Do you think Shane's career change has anything to do with the way God untangles his knots? Why or why not?
- What have you given up to be here with this group? Why?
- Knowing what good things you're sacrificing to be here, why are you here?

SHANE HIPPS CAME TO MINISTRY FROM THE WORLD HIGH-END ADVERTISING, SO IT'S NOT SURPRISING TH HE HAS A KNACK FOR UNPACKING THE DEEPER LAYE OF THE GOSPEL MESSAGE. FOR SHANE, THERE IS MO TO OUR IDEAS ABOUT SALVATION THAN JUST WHAT HAPPENS AFTER WE DIE. HE SAYS, "SALVATION IS NO JUST A ONE-TIME PROMISE FOR WHEN WE DIE. IT'S A MOMENT-BY-MOMENT POSSIBILITY WHILE WE LIVE.

MORE SHANE TRIVIA
- TEACHING PASTOR AT MARS HILL BIBLE CHURCH IN GRAND RAPIDS, MICHIGAN, WHICH MEETS IN A FORMER SUPERMARKET
- WORKED AS AN ADVERTISING EXECUTIVE ON ACCOUNTS LIKE GUINNESS AND PORSCHE
- WENT TO SEMINARY AS A CALVINIST AND IS NOW A MENNONITE
- WEARS VIBRAM FIVE FINGERS WHEN HE RUNS
- BA FROM TEXAS CHRISTIAN UNIVERSITY
- MDIV FROM FULLER THEOLOGICAL SEMINARY

SHANE'S BOOKS:
- FLICKERING PIXELS: HOW TECHNOLOGY SHAPES YOUR FAITH
- SELLING WATER BY THE RIVER: A BOOK ABOUT THE LIFE JESUS AND THE RELIGION THAT GETS IN THE WAY

58 **animate**

IN JOHN 6, AFTER A CONFRONTATION BETWEEN JESUS AND THE AUTHORITIES, DISCIPLES START TO LEAVE JESUS' GROUP. HE ASKS HIS TWELVE, "DO YOU WANT TO GO AWAY AS WELL?" BUT PETER ANSWERS, "LORD, TO WHOM SHALL WE GO? YOU HAVE THE WORDS OF ETERNAL LIFE" (JOHN 6:66-68). CONCLUSION: WHATEVER YOU GAVE UP TO BE HERE AT ANIMATE, YOU ARE IN THE RIGHT PLACE!

QUESTIONS OF
SALVATION HAVE
BEEN AT THE
FOREFRONT
OF CHRISTIAN
CONVERSATION FOR
GENERATIONS. WE
CONTINUE TO ASK
OURSELVES BIG
QUESTIONS ABOUT
HOW WE ARE SAVED
AND WHAT PART, IF
ANY, WE PLAY IN OUR
OWN SALVATION.
WHAT DO YOU THINK?

SALVATION SOMETHING
WE CAN GAIN AND LOSE?

SALVATION A GIFT?
HOW IS IT GIVEN, RECEIVED?

SAVED!
17862 ms
GLORIFIED
SANCTIFIED
JUSTIFIED
TRIED-TO-ABIDE
HOGTIED
CHICKEN-FRIED
CONVICTIFIED
FREEZE-DRIED
BACKSLIDE
CLANG!
HRRGH!

SHANE HIPPS SAYS THAT WHEN JESUS WAS
TALKING ABOUT ETERNAL LIFE, THE KINGDOM
OF GOD, OR THE KINGDOM OF HEAVEN, HE
MOST OFTEN USED THE PRESENT TENSE.

SALVATION: ABUNDANT LIFE NOW | SHANE HIPPS ○○○○○○ 59

In the video, Shane invites people
into rethinking the salvation of God.
Talk about stereotypes such as of preachers
who offer salvation, like tent revivalists and
televangelists. There are also some pretty negative
(and sometimes well-deserved) attitudes. Perhaps
some in your group have experienced these personally.
• What are some positive and negative affects
of popular teachings about salvation?
• If you were to take a whack at the "Salvation"
carnival game, how high would your "dinger" rise?
• How well does this illustration line up
with typical views on salvation?
• How do passages like James 2:14-26 challenge
the stereotypes about salvation?

Read the story of Zacchaeus
in Luke 19:1-11. Invite your group to
sing "Zacchaeus Was a Wee Little Man" if
they know it. Laugh about "a wee little man"
and other lyrics of this silly song. Then notice
that "salvation" comes up here. Jesus says,
"Today salvation has come to this house."
• What does he mean?
• When does salvation seem to start
happening in this story?
• Do you think Zacchaeus gained future
salvation by changing his practices? Or is
the response of Zacchaeus really
what Jesus meant when he
talked about salvation?

ZACCHAEUS WAS A "CHIEF TAX COLLECTOR," OR A
PERSON WHO BOUGHT RIGHTS FROM THE ROMAN
EMPIRE TO GOUGE THE JEWISH PEOPLE DURING
COLLECTION. HE DID THIS THROUGH A TEAM OF
REGULAR TAX COLLECTORS. (THINK OF THIS
LIKE THE HEAD OF A PRIVATE WASTE REMOVAL
COMPANY AND HER/HIS INDIVIDUAL GARBAGE
COLLECTORS.) THAT'S WHY HE WAS "VERY RICH."

Sarah Rollens writes, "Greek authors, Roman authors, rabbinic writings, and even ancient documentary papyri demonstrate that
tax-collectors were routinely despised . . ." ("Jesus and the Tax-Collectors: Relative Deprivation and Status Crystallization among the
Followers of Jesus," in *Prandium: Journal of Historical Studies*, http://jps.library.utoronto.ca/index.php/prandium/article/view/16218).

USING A MAZE ILLUSTRATION,

this spread features Jesus' stated purpose from Isaiah 61 and Luke 4. The word salvation is not in these passages, but the message offered in them contrasts an "after death" fixation on salvation with what Jesus brings to the world. Invite the group to meditatively work the maze, before animating the conversation.

What does salvation in this life look like? Feel like? Sound like? Shane compares it to the untangling of a knotted rope, the calm at the eye of the hurricane, the best course in a feast. The Journal urges us to find an alternative path toward an understanding of salvation.
• How do you picture God's salvation now?
• What are God moments like?
• Epiphanies, spiritual and emotional relief, a full experience of life—can these really be what Jesus meant by salvation? Why or why not?
• Add some of your impressions of salvation to the maze.

This maze is full of dead ends when it comes to the doctrine of salvation. We can totally focus on NOT going there, but Jesus has a completely different focus for salvation in mind. When Jesus described his saving work by quoting from Isaiah, he offered us five ways to "work out" (Philippians 2:12b) our salvation in the here and now: good news to the poor, release to the captives, sight to the blind, freedom to the oppressed, the Jubilee year for everybody.
• How do these five matter to you?
• Should you read the conditions literally? Or spiritually? Why?
• Do you see yourself helped here? How?
• How do these five matter for the community around you? For people around the world?
• Does it feel like Jesus is describing other people or all of us? Why?

THEOLOGIANS, ARTISTS, WRITERS, AND CHRISTIANS OF ALL STRIPES HAVE SPENT CENTURIES TRYING TO FIGURE OUT WHAT SALVATION IS REALLY ABOUT. THE IDEAS THAT HAVE COME FROM ALL THAT EFFORT ARE OFTEN HELPFUL, BUT SOMETIMES THEY ARE SO COMPELLING THAT THEY KEEP US FROM EXPLORING OTHER IDEAS.

START HERE

PEARLY GATES

SHANE ASKS US TO MAKE OUR WAY BACK TO WHAT JESUS HAD TO SAY ABOUT SALVATION. WHAT DO JESUS' WORDS SUGGEST?

SHANE BELIEVES THAT SALVATION HAS AT LEAST AS MUCH TO WITH THIS LIFE AS THE NEXT. WHAT DO YOU THINK ABOUT THA

50 animate

IN LUKE 4, JESUS IDENTIFIES HIMSELF AS THE "ONE" ISAIAH 61 WAS TALKING ABOUT. THE DISTANCE BETWEEN JESUS' SELF-UNDERSTANDING (AUTHORITATIVE VOICE AND AGENT OF GOD) AND THE NAZARENES' ESTIMATE OF HIM (JOSEPH'S LITTLE BOY) ULTIMATELY GETS HIM INTO TROUBLE. IN LUKE, WE READ: "WHEN THEY HEARD THIS, ALL IN THE SYNAGOGUE WERE FILLED WITH RAGE. THEY GOT UP, DROVE HIM OUT OF THE TOWN, AND LED HIM TO THE BROW OF THE HILL ON WHICH THEIR TOWN WAS BUILT, SO THAT THEY MIGHT HURL HIM OFF THE CLIFF." (LUKE 4:28-29) OF COURSE, HE GOT AWAY, AS IT SAYS IN VERSE 30: "BUT HE PASSED THROUGH THE MIDST OF THEM AND WENT ON HIS WAY." AMAZING.

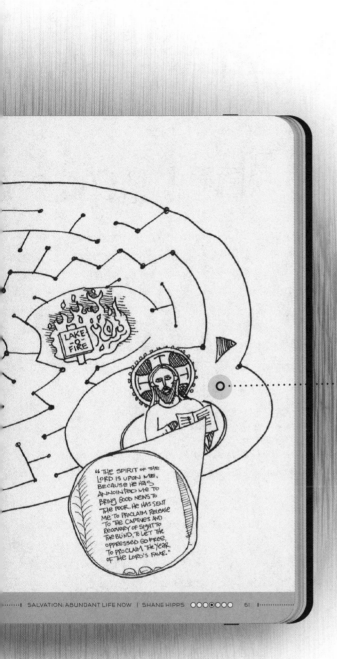

Jesus and Salvation. Have your group flip through the Gospels to find salvation scenes. If you get stuck, try these:
• A Samaritan woman who has just spoken with Jesus tells her townspeople, "Come and see a man who told me everything I have ever done! He cannot be the Messiah, can he?" (John 4:29)
• A woman who was caught in adultery is rescued from a stoning and Jesus does not condemn her (John 8:10-11)
• Jesus describes new birth to Nicodemus (John 3:1-10)
• Jesus retraces the steps of Peter's three denials by asking three times if Peter loves him (John 21:15-19)
• Are these moments of salvation? Why or why not?

JESUS CHOSE THE "YEAR OF JUBILEE" AS THE FINAL IMAGE TO DESCRIBE THE KIND OF SALVATION THAT GOD SENT HIM TO BRING. THE IMAGERY COMES FROM LEVITICUS 25. THIS LAW OF MOSES DECLARES THAT EVERY 50TH YEAR, SLAVES SHOULD BE RELEASED, DEBTS SHOULD BE FORGIVEN AND LAND SHOULD BE RETURNED TO ITS ORIGINAL OWNERS. SHANE DRAWS ON THIS IMAGE FOR HIS UNDERSTANDING OF SALVATION AS LIBERATION IN THE HERE AND NOW.

"FOR JESUS, SALVATION IS HERE AND NOW JUST AS MUCH
AS IT IS THERE AND THEN." —SHANE HIPPS

Talk about what it means for us
as modern day Christians that there
are so many references to salvation in the
Old Testament (pre-Jesus and pre-beliefs
about an afterlife). Have the group open their
Bibles to the verses quoted in the Journal.
  • What did "salvation" mean in
      each of these passages?
• Compare these Old Testament ideas of salvation
   to salvation as it appears in Luke 1:77, Acts
    13:47, Romans 1:16, as examples. What
      is the meaning of salvation in these
           New Testament places?

AROUND TWO-THIRDS OF "SALVATION"
APPEARANCES IN THE BIBLE COME IN
THE OLD TESTAMENT. THERE ARE OVER
50 REFERENCES IN PSALMS ALONE.

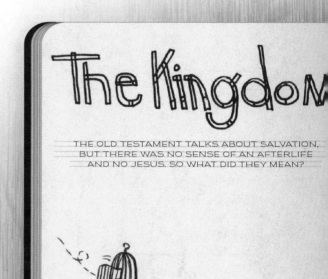

The Kingdom

THE OLD TESTAMENT TALKS ABOUT SALVATION,
BUT THERE WAS NO SENSE OF AN AFTERLIFE
AND NO JESUS. SO WHAT DID THEY MEAN?

EXODUS 15:2:
THE LORD IS MY
STRENGTH AND
MY MIGHT, AND
HE HAS BECOME
MY SALVATION;
THIS IS MY GOD,
AND I WILL
PRAISE HIM,
MY FATHER'S
GOD, AND I WILL
EXALT HIM.

2 CHRONICLES 6:41:
LET YOUR
PRIESTS, O LORD
GOD, BE CLOTHED
WITH SALVATION,
AND LET YOUR
FAITHFUL
REJOICE IN YOUR
GOODNESS.

PSALM 27:1:
THE LORD
IS MY LIGHT
AND MY
SALVATION;
WHOM SHALL
I FEAR? THE
LORD IS THE
STRONGHOLD
OF MY LIFE;
OF WHOM
SHALL I BE
AFRAID?

PSALM 62:5-6:
FOR GOD ALONE
MY SOUL WAITS
IN SILENCE, FOR
MY HOPE IS
FROM HIM. HE
ALONE IS
MY ROCK AND
MY SALVATION,
MY FORTRESS;
I SHALL NOT
BE SHAKEN.

20763

| 62   animate

ONE OF THE MOST POPULAR HYMNS IN HISTORY
EXPLORES THE WONDER OF ETERNAL AFTERLIFE IN
THIS WAY: "WHEN WE'VE BEEN THERE 10,000 YEARS,
BRIGHT SHINING AS THE SUN, WE'VE NO LESS DAYS
TO SING GOD'S PRAISE THAN WHEN WE'VE FIRST
BEGUN." (JOHN NEWTON, "AMAZING GRACE")

C.S. Lewis writes, "Our life comes to us moment by moment. One moment disappears before the next comes along: and there is room for very
little in each. That is what Time is like. And of course you and I tend to take it for granted that this Time series—this arrangement of past,
present, and future—is not simply the way life comes to us but the way all things really exist. We tend to assume that the whole universe and
God Himself are always moving on from past to future just as we do . . . God, I believe, does not live in a Time-series at all. His life is not dribbled
out moment by moment like ours: with Him it is still 1920 and already 1960." (Mere Christianity, pp. 146–47)

WHEN YOU THINK OF SALVATION, DO YOU THINK OF IT
AS BEING SAVED FROM SOMETHING OR TO SOMETHING?

HOW DOES OUR SENSE OF SALVATION INFLUENCE
THE DECISIONS WE MAKE, THE LIFE WE LIVE NOW?

F YOU THOUGHT THIS WAS IT, WOULD YOU LIVE DIFFERENTLY?"

| SALVATION: ABUNDANT LIFE NOW | SHANE HIPPS ⦾⦾⦾⦾⦾⦿⦾ 63 |

There are several images of
release and rescue on this spread
in the Journal. Salvation can be just
that—a feeling of release or rescue.
• Do you think God is responsible for all our moments
of relief, rescue, and release? Why or why not?
• How have you experienced what a bird experiences
when it is freed from a cage? What a person
feels when he becomes unchained?
• How does that interplay with how you feel
when you think about Jesus defeating
death? For more on this see Hebrews
2:14-18 and Romans 8:31-39.
• Draw other images of salvation
in the Journal.

For many believers, salvation is
essentially the key to a good afterlife.
But Shane gives the afterlife very little
attention, and he even seems to subordinate
it to salvation in this life. The Journal asks
your group to place themselves in Shane's view
of the Kingdom of God. Ask your group, "How
do you feel about the idea that salvation is
about this life now?" Invite the group do do
more research on the phrases "Kingdom
of God" and "Kingdom of Heaven"
in the Bible and elsewhere.

SHANE'S CHARACTERIZATION COVERS MOST OF JESUS'
REFERENCES TO ETERNAL LIFE AND THE KINGDOM
OF GOD, LIKE LUKE 17:20-21. OTHER TIMES, THOUGH,
JESUS CLEARLY POINTS TO A FUTURE SALVATION
OR KINGDOM OR ETERNAL LIFE AFTER JESUS COMES
AGAIN, SUCH AS IN MARK 13:13 AND MATTHEW 25:31, 46.

GIVE YOUR GROUP PERMISSION
to share disagreements with Shane and with one another.
Who are the "both/and" people? The "next-life only" folks?
Is there a "this-life only" vote? Which salvation is more
important to them? Why? Can the two coexist peaceably?
Or will EITHER here-and-now OR there-and-then ultimately
win? This could be a lively conversation!

John Murawski's Huffington Post article: "N.T. Wright Asks: Have Christians Gotten Heaven All Wrong?" does a good job of exposing
popular misunderstandings about the Kingdom of God that have made their way into the Christian worldview (http://www.huffingtonpost.
com/2012/05/17/nt-wright-christian-heaven-is-wrong_n_1524117.html).

Many evangelists have used clocks very differently than Shane does: to count down the amount of time we have left to make a decision that will impact our afterlife. In other words, decision now, salvation later. Paul's words lend themselves to this: "Besides this, you know what time it is, how it is now the moment for you to wake from sleep. For salvation is nearer to us now than when we became believers; the night is far gone, the day is near." (Romans 13:11-12) Divide up the group to read 2 Corinthians 6:1-3; Ephesians 5:15,16; 1 Peter 4:7-11; 1 John 2:15-17.
• How do these passages link up the concept of time with salvation?
• In what ways do they inspire us to "do" something with our salvation here and now?"

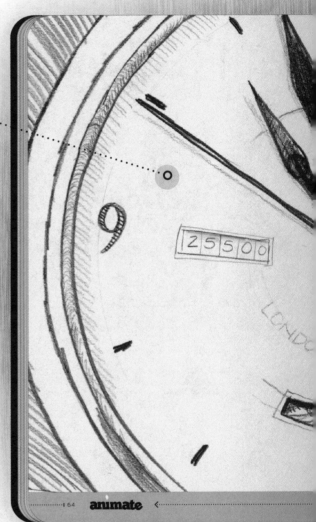

"DO WE RECOGNIZE THE MOMENTS OF SALVATION IN THIS LIFE? AND IF WE DON'T, WHAT MAKES US THINK WE'LL RECOGNIZE SALVATION IN THE NEXT? ARE WE WILLING TO WAKE UP TO THE POSSIBILITY THAT THE 25,550 DAYS WE HAVE ARE ACTUALLY THE MAIN COURSE?" —SHANE HIPPS

If you buy into Shane's idea that salvation is now, what actions do you take? Read Ephesians 4:26—5:2 together. Encourage group members to write some actions in their Journals. Ask them to sketch what they think it means to be "sealed for the day of redemption."
• When is the day of redemption? Now? Later? Or did we already miss it?
• How have you already seen salvation in your life? How will you recognize it in the future?

FUNNY TECHNICALITY: SHANE FORGOT LEAP YEARS. SEVENTY LIVED YEARS INCLUDE 17 OR 18 EXTRA DAYS, SO, TO QUOTE BILL MURRAY IN CADDYSHACK, "WE GOT THAT GOIN' FOR US, WHICH IS NICE."

"THE ETERNAL LIFE JESUS PROMISED CAN START NOW AND NEVER HAS TO END . . . IT'S A CHOICE WE MAKE NOW, TO TRUST JESUS AND EXPERIENCE A PLACE WITHIN US OF UNFOLDING LOVE, OF BOUNDLESS PEACE, OF INDESTRUCTIBLE JOY . . . MAYBE YOU'VE EXPERIENCED THAT KIND OF SALVATION . . . MAYBE YOU'R LONGING FOR THAT RIGHT NOW." —SHANE HIPPS

IF YOUR GROUP MEMBERS TRUST one another enough to risk sharing, this activity will rock! If not, you may want to have them draw or write their Before and After thinking into their Journals. It's possible that some of your group will choose to share publicly while others will keep theirs private.

Before and After.
In advance, prepare a big slab of cardboard for each person in the group. Provide big markers. Invite your group to quietly contemplate one moment when they experienced a feeling of salvation like Shane did when the knot in his chest released or when he was in the eye of the hurricane. Have them write that experience in code on one side of the cardboard. Then ask them whether they experienced salvation—a sense of God's rescue or change—in that moment. Have them write that experience in code on the other side. If they did not experience salvation, they can leave the second side blank. When everyone is done, put on good music about the love of God and invite all members of the group to show the before and after of their experience to everyone.
• What did you feel during your experience?
• Where do you think God was during this experience?
• How do you think your experience relates to salvation?
• What changed after your experience?
• What does "eternal life now not later" mean for you?

For some the ticking clock of this-life feels like a nightmare out of a Dicken's novel. The tyranny of time wants to make slaves of us all. Schedules, calendars, deadlines abound. Shane's message that we would grasp God's gift of eternal love in the here-and-now is liberating. Between sessions look for clues that God is directing "your moments and your days" as the old hymn says, into ways that can redeem time itself.

Before and After might look like this: http://www.youtube.com/watch?v=eYqblUuiNhg&feature=share

CROSS | WHERE GOD IS
NADIA BOLZ-WEBER

WHAT IS IT ABOUT US THAT MAKES US ALWAYS CHOOSE
THE BEDAZZLED CROSS AND NOT THE ACTUAL ONE?

In the last session, Shane Hipps introduced some different ways to think about salvation. Now, Nadia offers her take on the cross and how we might make sense of what was accomplished by the crucifixion of Jesus. Nadia asks us to think about how our interpretation of the cross lines up with our understanding of God.

MAKE THIS WEEK'S TOPIC—THE CROSS—

obvious. Fill the meeting space with a variety of crosses. Announce BYOC (Bring Your Own Cross) by texting or emailing the group ahead of time. Have songs about the cross playing as people arrive. Ideas include, "By the Marks" by Gillian Welch, "The Beautiful, Terrible Cross" by Selah, or the traditional hymn "Lift High the Cross."

You'll see in the video that Nadia talks about lots of different crosses— the cross Jesus died on, the ornate crosses the church created, and everything in between. She asks a tough question: "How [did] an instrument of death and torture in the Roman Empire . . . have anything to do with a loving God?" Talk about images of the cross with your group.
• What comes to mind when you think about the cross? Images? Music? Feelings? Situations?
• What are some unusual places you've seen a cross?
• Read Nadia's quote to the group. Reactions? Perhaps the truly unusual place is a cheap jewelry rack in a discount store!

To get to know who Nadia is, follow the tats. She has images of the cross and Luther's Latin phrase *simul justus et peccator*, which means "simultaneously righteous and a sinner." Nadia's church is called "House of All Saints and Sinners." Notice a pattern?
• How do Nadia's tattoo images relate to each other?
• If you were going to get a tattoo representing your belief about the cross, what would it look like? Sketch it in your Journal.
• Why might someone start a church called "House of All Saints and Sinners"?
• If you could start a church, what would you call it and why?

"I CAME TO THE CHRISTIAN FAITH BY A TWISTED ROAD . . . IT TOOK ME TEN YEARS, A NAGGING CHEMICAL ABUSE PROBLEM, AND A CUTE NEW LUTHERAN BOYFRIEND FOR ME TO COME BACK TO THE CHRISTIAN FAITH." –NADIA BOLZ-WEBER

CROSS ⋯⋯> Chapter 7 of Paul's letter to the Romans played big with Luther, especially Romans 7:19: "The good that I wish I do not do, but I practice the very evil that I do not wish." Interpreters continue to debate whether Paul was portraying himself as a Christian (Luther's view) or speaking the frustration of someone who has not yet embraced Christ or received God's Spirit (John Wesley's view).

NADIA CHALLENGES TWO VIEWS OF THE cross that are central to many Christians' faith. This may fly in the face of your beliefs or the beliefs of your group members. If objections arise, direct the conversation toward healthy debate. Asking questions, disagreeing, and looking for answers are central to journeying in faith.

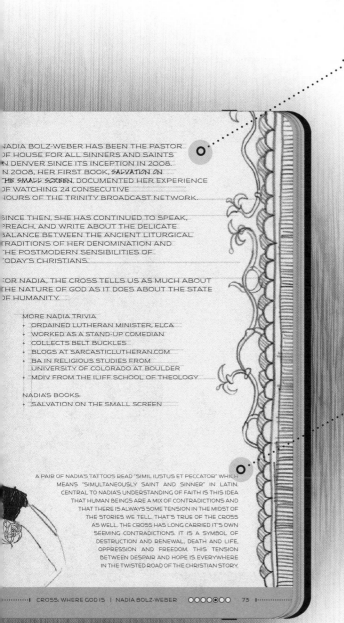

NADIA BOLZ-WEBER HAS BEEN THE PASTOR OF HOUSE FOR ALL SINNERS AND SAINTS IN DENVER SINCE ITS INCEPTION IN 2008. IN 2008, HER FIRST BOOK, *SALVATION ON THE SMALL SCREEN*, DOCUMENTED HER EXPERIENCE OF WATCHING 24 CONSECUTIVE HOURS OF THE TRINITY BROADCAST NETWORK.

SINCE THEN, SHE HAS CONTINUED TO SPEAK, PREACH, AND WRITE ABOUT THE DELICATE BALANCE BETWEEN THE ANCIENT LITURGICAL TRADITIONS OF HER DENOMINATION AND THE POSTMODERN SENSIBILITIES OF TODAY'S CHRISTIANS.

FOR NADIA, THE CROSS TELLS US AS MUCH ABOUT THE NATURE OF GOD AS IT DOES ABOUT THE STATE OF HUMANITY.

MORE NADIA TRIVIA
+ ORDAINED LUTHERAN MINISTER, ELCA
+ WORKED AS A STAND-UP COMEDIAN
+ COLLECTS BELT BUCKLES
+ BLOGS AT SARCASTICLUTHERAN.COM
+ BA IN RELIGIOUS STUDIES FROM UNIVERSITY OF COLORADO AT BOULDER
+ MDIV FROM THE ILIFF SCHOOL OF THEOLOGY

NADIA'S BOOKS:
+ SALVATION ON THE SMALL SCREEN

A PAIR OF NADIA'S TATTOOS READ "SIMIL IUSTUS ET PECCATOR" WHICH MEANS "SIMULTANEOUSLY SAINT AND SINNER" IN LATIN. CENTRAL TO NADIA'S UNDERSTANDING OF FAITH IS THIS IDEA THAT HUMAN BEINGS ARE A MIX OF CONTRADICTIONS AND THAT THERE IS ALWAYS SOME TENSION IN THE MIDST OF THE STORIES WE TELL. THAT'S TRUE OF THE CROSS AS WELL. THE CROSS HAS LONG CARRIED IT'S OWN SEEMING CONTRADICTIONS. IT IS A SYMBOL OF DESTRUCTION AND RENEWAL, DEATH AND LIFE, OPPRESSION AND FREEDOM. THIS TENSION BETWEEN DESPAIR AND HOPE IS EVERYWHERE IN THE TWISTED ROAD OF THE CHRISTIAN STORY.

Read Romans 6:1-14 together. This passage connects the cross with baptism. Martin Luther said, "The Old Adam in each of us is a pretty strong swimmer and is not easily drowned in the waters of baptism." What does this mean? Our sinfulness is with us our whole lives. Being baptized doesn't make us sin-free. Encourage group members to write this quote in their Journals. Talk about the quote together.
• When have you felt like Old Adam or Eve was sitting in the Devil's place on your shoulder?
• Draw a chart, graph, or sketch representing the levels of sinner and saint you see within yourself.

LUTHER MENTIONED THE PHRASE "SIMUL JUSTUS ET PECCATOR" AS EARLY AS 1515, TWO YEARS BEFORE HE POSTED THE 95 THESES. SEVERAL YEARS LATER IN A TREATISE OF 1521 CALLED "AGAINST LATOMUS," HE DEVELOPED THE CONCEPT BY ARGUING THAT WE ARE NOT JUSTIFIED BY OUR "INNER RIGHTEOUSNESS" BUT BY CHRIST'S RIGHTEOUSNESS. LUTHER BELIEVED THAT OUR SINFULNESS REMAINS WITH US THROUGHOUT OUR LIVES.

"In 1517 in the little university town of Wittenberg, Germany, a Roman Catholic Monk named Martin Luther proposed ninety-five statements for debate about the Christian faith." Rolf Jacobson goes on to assert in *Crazy Talk: A Not So Stuffy Dictionary of Theological Terms* (Minneapolis, Minn.: Augsburg Books, 2008) that by doing so Martin Luther started "a revolution in Christianity" that is "still happening."

Watch the video together.
Leave a couple quiet minutes after
it ends for the group to write or sketch
in the Journal, or just think. Then talk
together about Nadia's point of view.
• What three pictures of God does Nadia paint?
• Which picture of God do you most relate to?
• Have you always thought of God that way or
did you used to view God differently? How so?
• How is thinking of "God on the cross" different
from thinking of "God above the cross"?
• How does seeing God in the cradle
and on the cross communicate
to you who God is?

Check out these representations of the cross:

Legend has it that the night before the Battle of Milvian Bridge
in October of the year 312 C.E., Constantine was commanded in
a dream to "delineate the heavenly sign on the shields of his soldiers."
(Lactantius, On the Deaths of the Persecutors 44.5) The "heavenly
sign" was a staurogram—the Latin cross. Constantine won the battle and
sole reign over the Roman Empire, becoming its first Christian emperor.

The Apostle Paul wrote in Galatians 2:20, "I have been crucified with Christ, and it is
no longer I who live but Christ lives in me." St. Francis of Assisi physically experienced
that co-crucifixion Paul pictured. In 1224, during a time of fasting, he experienced the
physical signs of the cross (stigmata) being pierced through his wrists and feet.

In 1915, Thomas Dixon's novel, Birth of a Nation, described a burning cross
as summons to an errand of life and death. The same year, a Jewish man named
Leo Frank was lynched in Marietta, Georgia. Two months later, the lynch mob
burned a cross in celebration. Not long after that, William Simmons burned
a cross on a mountaintop to signal the beginning of the Ku Klux Klan.

The swastika did not start as a variation on the cross. It began as a
Sanskrit symbol meaning "to be good." It appealed to German nationalists in the late
1800s because of Aryan associations. Even American soldiers wore it during WWI. Then
Hitler's use of it for anti-Semitic purposes of the Nazi Party changed everything.

Divvy these up among your group and have them respond to each
representation of the cross. Take some time to discuss:
• What are some other representations of the cross you've seen?
How have they affected how you felt about who God is?
• If the cross was used to represent you, what would it mean?
• How do you work to live "in the name of Christ"?

THE CROSS
HAD BEEN A
SYMBOL OF
THE CHRISTIAN
CHURCH SINCE
THE DEATH AND
RESURRECTION
OF JESUS. BUT
LIKE SO MUCH
IN THE WINDING,
TANGLED
CHRITSTIAN
STORY, IT
HAS BEEN
INTERPRETED
IN VASTLY
DIFFERENT WAYS.
IT HAS BEEN
ENCRUSTED
WITH JEWELS
TO SHOW THE
WEALTH AND
POWER OF THE
CHURCH, HELD
AT THE HEAD
OF ADVANCING
ARMIES
FIGHTING IN THE
NAME OF GOD,
AND TWISTED
INTO AN ALMOST
UNRECOGNIZABLE
FORM BY THE
NAZIS. YET
EVEN WHEN
IT'S MANGLED
AND MISUSED,
IT REMAINS
A POWERFUL
SYMBOL.

AS YOU LOOK AT THES
CROSSES: WHICH ONE
ARE YOU DRAWN TO?
WHICH ONES FEEL
WEIRD OR COMFORTIN
OR REPULSIVE?

IF YOU WERE TO ADD A
ADJECTIVE TO EACH O
THESE CROSSES, WHA
WOULD YOU WRITE?

WHEN WE
REALLY LOOK,
WE SEE WHO
GOD IS IN HOW
GOD CHOSE TO
REVEAL GOD'S
SELF IN A
CRADLE AND
ON a CROSS

—NADIA BOLZ-WEBER

74   animate

Look at the variety of crosses in the Journal and in the room. Take a tour of your church building or ask group members to recall what crosses they've seen in the church. As a group, assign an adjective to each cross. It's OK to be off the wall. For example, the pastel colored resin cross could be "morbid," given it's placement in the church nursery.
• How did you decide which adjective to give each cross?
• What does it mean when someone wears or displays a cross?
• Picture a rap star wearing a big, gold, bejeweld cross on a necklace. Then picture a cross made out of sticks like a camp counselor might wear. Write down two impressions you would have of each person. How did their cross affect how you felt? Which one seemed "right" to you?

"THE IRONY, OF COURSE, IS THAT JUST A COUPLE CENTURIES INTO THE CHRISTIAN FAITH, THE CHURCH ALIGNED ITSELF WITH EMPIRE RATHER THAN OPPOSING IT, AND WE BEGAN TO RESEMBLE THE VERY FORCES THAT REJECTED CHRIST IN THE FIRST PLACE. AND THIS WOULD ALSO BE THE POINT IN HISTORY WHEN WE ENCRUSTED CROSSES WITH GOLD AND JEWELS AS IF WE'RE TRYING TO MASK THE FOOLISHNESS OF A GOD WHO SUFFERS AND DIES."
—NADIA BOLZ-WEBER

THE CROSSES ON THIS PAGE ALL HAVE BAGGAGE.

Some good, some bad, most both. From celtic cross to crucifix, from Iron Cross to the cross pressed into communion wafers, these images say more about us than they do about God. Nadia is intentionally deconstructing this symbol. However, be mindful that symbols have power, as do the ideas they convey. Group members may take issue with Nadia—that's OK. Remember the goal is not total agreement but animated conversation.

What's the cross without the crucifixion of Jesus? As a group, read through Jesus' crucifixion in one or more of the Gospels. You can find the story in Mark 15:33-39, Matthew 27:45-56, Luke 23:26-49, and John 19:18-30. If possible, consider showing a clip from a film such as *Jesus of Nazareth* or *Jesus* (the Campus Crusade for Christ film). Ask the group to share their reactions to these crucifixion scenes.

GUSTAV AULEN (1879-1977) REINTRODUCED THE "CHRISTUS VICTOR" THEORY OF ATONEMENT TO THE TWENTIETH CENTURY IN HIS BOOK OF THAT TITLE, PUBLISHED IN 1921. HE ARGUED THAT CV HAD DOMINATED CHRISTIAN THOUGHT FOR ITS FIRST 1,000 YEARS AND OUGHT TO BE RECLAIMED.

ORIGEN OF ALEXANDRIA WAS ONE OF THE MOST BRILLIANT EARLY CHRISTIANS, ABLE TO HOLD HIS OWN WITH THE HEAVYWEIGHT MINDS OF ALEXANDRIA. HE SPELLS OUT HIS RANSOM THEORY IN *AGAINST CELSUS* 7.17. CHRIST GIVES HIS LIFE AS A RANSOM TO THE DEVIL, WHO HAS HELD HUMANITY CAPTIVE SINCE ADAM AND EVE'S FALL.

GREGORY OF NYSSA (335-395) WAS AMONG THE "CAPPADOCIAN FATHERS" OF THE CHURCH (PRESENT-DAY TURKEY). HE ARGUED THE THEORY THAT LATER BECAME KNOWN AS "CHRISTUS VICTOR" IN HIS CATECHETICAL ORATIONS.

PETER ABELARD (1079-1142) TAUGHT THAT CHRIST ACCOMPLISHED ATONEMENT THROUGH HIS MORAL INFLUENCE ON HUMANITY. ABELARD'S EMPHASIS ON THE LIFE AND TEACHING OF JESUS WIDENS OUR FOCUS FROM THE CROSS ALONE TO ALL THE OTHER WAYS THAT JESUS LIVED OUT LOVE FOR THE WORLD. THE CROSS IS THE CULMINATION OF A LIFE LIVED FOR OTHERS.

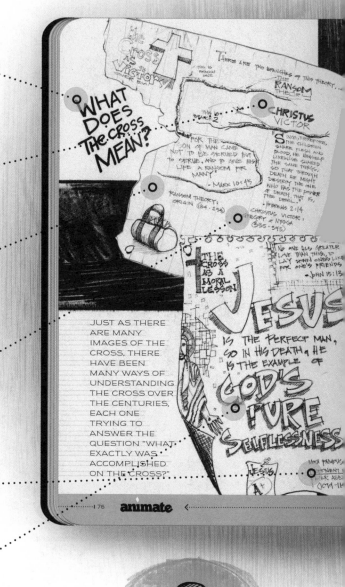

"

"[IT'S LIKE GOD SAID], 'HERE'S THE EXTENT I WILL GO TO DEFY YOUR IDEA OF ME AS A VENGEFUL GOD: I WON'T EVEN LIFT A FINGER TO CONDEMN THE PEOPLE WHO HUNG ME . . . I WOULD RATHER DIE THAN BE IN THE SIN-ACCOUNTING BUSINESS ANYMORE.'" —NADIA BOLZ-WEBER

"

Compare this quote to the Psalm 51—a text that is assigned to be read on Ash Wednesday.

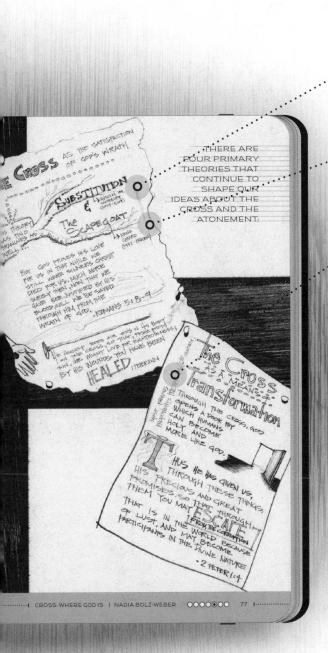

THERE ARE FOUR PRIMARY THEORIES THAT CONTINUE TO SHAPE OUR IDEAS ABOUT THE CROSS AND THE ATONEMENT:

ANSELM OF CANTERBURY (1033-1109) INTRODUCED THE THEORY OF SUBSTITUTIONARY ATONEMENT IN HIS *CUR DEUS HOMO*. HE PICTURES HUMANITY OWING GOD A HUGE DEBT OF HONOR BECAUSE WE HAVE FAILED TO WORSHIP AND LIVE IN THE LIGHT OF GOD. CHRIST'S DEATH PAYS THE DEBT.

RENE GIRARD (1932-PRESENT) SEES THE DEATH OF JESUS AS A REVERSAL OF THE HUMAN PRACTICE OF SCAPEGOATING IN ORDER TO DIFFUSE THE PRESSURE OF RIVALRY. JESUS WILLINGLY BECAME THE SCAPEGOAT AND SO REVERSED THE CYCLE.

IRENAEUS (CA 200) WAS THE BISHOP OF WHAT IS NOW LYONS, FRANCE. FOR IRENEAUS THE CROSS WAS THE CULMINATION OF A PROCESS BY WHICH GOD REDEEMED A CORRUPTED RELATIONSHIP WITH HUMANITY. GOD, IN THE PERSON OF CHRIST, TRANSFUSED DIVINE LIFE INTO EVERY STAGE OF HUMAN EXISTENCE—FROM BIRTH TO DEATH.

THERE ARE FOUR MAIN VIEWS

of the cross (atonement theories) presented in this spread. In some ways Nadia's views are in line with these theories, but in other ways her ideas create some tension. Before class, think about where Nadia's views fit in with these four categories so you can better help your group do the same.

Talk through the four ideas on this spread together. Then review Nadia's three images of God as represented through the cross: Angry Daddy, Accountant, and God-on-the-Cross. Work together to decide where these three ideas best fit on the diagram in the Journal. Write each idea in the appropriate place. Talk together.
• How do Nadia's ideas about the cross fit in or go against these four main ideas?
• How do you think Nadia's journey back to Christianity affected her view of the cross?
• How does your journey affect how you see the cross?
• Do you think there's a right answer? Why or why not?
• Which view or views of the cross most align with your view? Mark them in your Journal using symbols, lines, or whatever best represents your beliefs.

"JESUS HAD TO DIE BECAUSE HIS DAD WAS MAD AT US. IN THIS WAY OF THINKING, WE'RE BORN BAD AND CAN'T BE 100% GOOD BUT SHOULD TRY REALLY HARD ANYWAY AND THEN FEEL GUILTY FOR OUR INEVITABLE FAILURES, SINCE OUR FAILURES ARE THE REASON JESUS HAD TO DIE . . . JESUS IS SORT OF A SUPPORTING CHARACTER IN THIS ABUSIVE DRAMA BETWEEN GOD AND HUMANITY."
—NADIA BOLZ WEBER

Nadia argues against the "Angry Daddy" view of God that requires Jesus to die on the cross so God won't take out God's wrath on the rest of us. Throw this idea out to the group: is God ever angry? Have group members make a list in their Journals of things that might/do/should anger God. Talk about it.
• How do you think God feels about things like the holocaust, genocide, exploitation, and slavery?
• What is the difference between God's anger at these kinds of injustices and God's enduring anger at each individual (that would require Jesus to be punished in humanity's place)?
• What do you think is the relationship between love and anger in God?

IN ROMANS 1:18, PAUL TALKS ABOUT HOW "THE WRATH OF GOD" HAS BEEN REVEALED AGAINST HUMAN UNGODLINESS AND UNRIGHTEOUSNESS THAT SUPPRESSES TRUTH. GOD'S ANGER IS THEN A RESPONSE TO MISREPRESTATION!

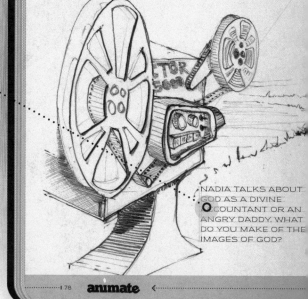

THE DISCUSSIONS ABOUT THE CROSS ARE REALLY DISCUSSIONS ABOUT THE NATURE OF GOD. THAT'S WHY THEY ARE DIFFICULT, EVEN TUMULTUOUS, CONVERSATIONS WITHIN THE CHURCH. THE CONFLICT COMES BACK TO THIS DICHOTOMY WE FIND IN SO MUCH OF OUR FAITH. IS GOD LOVING OR VENGEFUL? IS IT POSSIBLE FOR GOD TO BE BOTH?

NADIA TALKS ABOUT GOD AS A DIVINE ACCOUNTANT OR AN ANGRY DADDY. WHAT DO YOU MAKE OF THE IMAGES OF GOD?

animate

"THE CROSS IS LIKE A LEGAL TRANSACTION BETWEEN US AND GOD. THINK OF A HEAVENLY LEDGER WHERE IT TRACKS ALL THE TIMES WE'RE BAD AND THEN PUTS A DOLLAR AMOUNT NEXT TO THEM. AND THEN THE FINAL COLUMN IS HOW MUCH WE OWE GOD ONCE ALL THESE SINS ARE TALLIED. WELL, THE TOTAL IN THE FINAL COLUMN IS JUST WAY TOO BIG FOR US TO EVER PAY IT OFF. . . . AND, WELL, SOMEONE'S GOT TO PAY IT OFF . . . THE ONE GUY WHO NEVER ADDED TO THE TALLY BECAUSE HE DIDN'T SIN." —NADIA BOLZ-WEBER

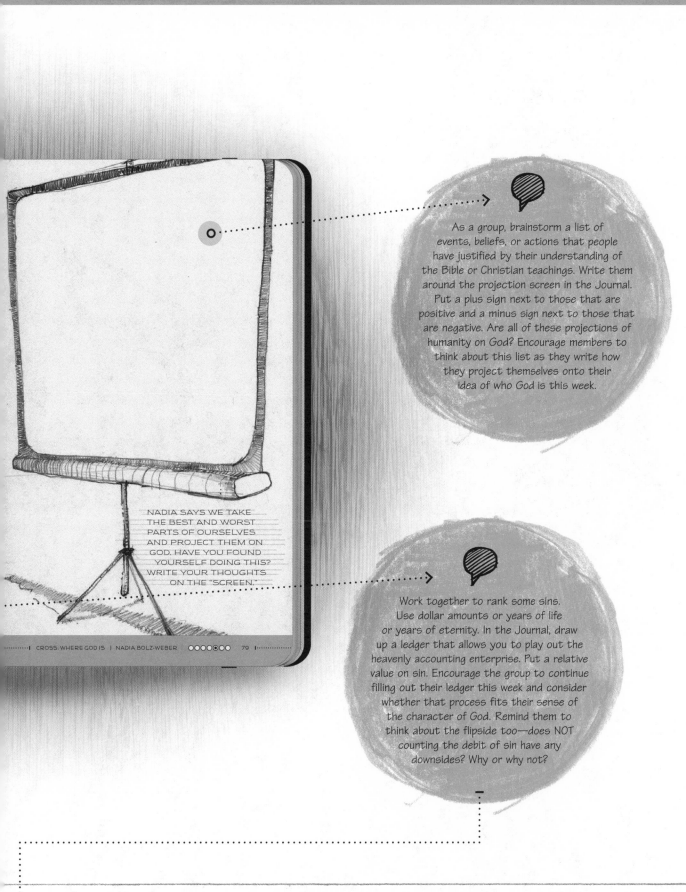

NADIA SAYS WE TAKE THE BEST AND WORST PARTS OF OURSELVES AND PROJECT THEM ON GOD. HAVE YOU FOUND YOURSELF DOING THIS? WRITE YOUR THOUGHTS ON THE "SCREEN."

CROSS: WHERE GOD IS | NADIA BOLZ-WEBER 79

As a group, brainstorm a list of events, beliefs, or actions that people have justified by their understanding of the Bible or Christian teachings. Write them around the projection screen in the Journal. Put a plus sign next to those that are positive and a minus sign next to those that are negative. Are all of these projections of humanity on God? Encourage members to think about this list as they write how they project themselves onto their idea of who God is this week.

Work together to rank some sins. Use dollar amounts or years of life or years of eternity. In the Journal, draw up a ledger that allows you to play out the heavenly accounting enterprise. Put a relative value on sin. Encourage the group to continue filling out their ledger this week and consider whether that process fits their sense of the character of God. Remind them to think about the flipside too—does NOT counting the debit of sin have any downsides? Why or why not?

The medieval church took this picture of a Divine Accountant to the extreme through the institution of indulgences. Acts of piety—prayers, acts of devotion, etc.—could each pay off a certain amount of debt. Even money could pay for sin. This is one of the parts of church life that drove Martin Luther to post his 95 Theses.

IN THE LAST SECTION OF HER TALK,

Nadia moves from what *God* has done for humanity through the cross to what *God* can do through Christians because we resemble the cross. Here, you can help the group transition to talking about the cruci-formational impact of the cross on Christians.

Whether around our necks, tattooed into our arms, on our altar, or in roadside shrines, the cross conveys a host of messages.
• Brainstorm as a group what might be different about the messages, given where diverse crosses are found.
• The real question is whether or not the message of the cross is enshrined in us. Divide up the group to read 1 Corinthians 1:18-21, 2 Corinthians 4:5-12, Galatians 2:15-21, Philippians 2:1-8, and Luke 9:18-26. Have them discuss and then share with the whole group what they believe their passage is saying about what it means to live a "cruciform" life.

ADD YOUR OWN ICONS TO THE ROADSIDE SHRINE.

animate

"WHILE WE MIGHT BE SEEKING A CHRISTIANITY BASED IN GLORY AND TRIUMPH, JESUS IS SEEKING US IN THE PLACES HE'S ALWAYS BEEN FOUND. NAMELY IN HUMAN FRAILTY, IN HUMAN BROKENNESS, IN THE UNWASHED MASSES. HE'S WOOING US IN SIMPLE TABLE FELLOWSHIP, AND CONTACT WITH THE UNCLEAN, AND CONFRONTING THE POWERS THAT BE. BECAUSE THE SHAPE OF CHRIST'S CHURCH IS . . . DECIDEDLY CRUCIFORM." —NADIA BOLZ-WEBER

CRU-CI-FORM. ADJ. SHAPED LIKE A CROSS; CRUCIATE.

For further reading on the character of God in the cross, see the classic book by Jürgen Moltmann, *The Crucified God*, (Minneapolis, Minn.: Fortress Press, 1993).

For a brief summary of each major theory of atonement, see Tony Jones' ebook, *A Better Atonement*, (The JoPa Group, 2012).

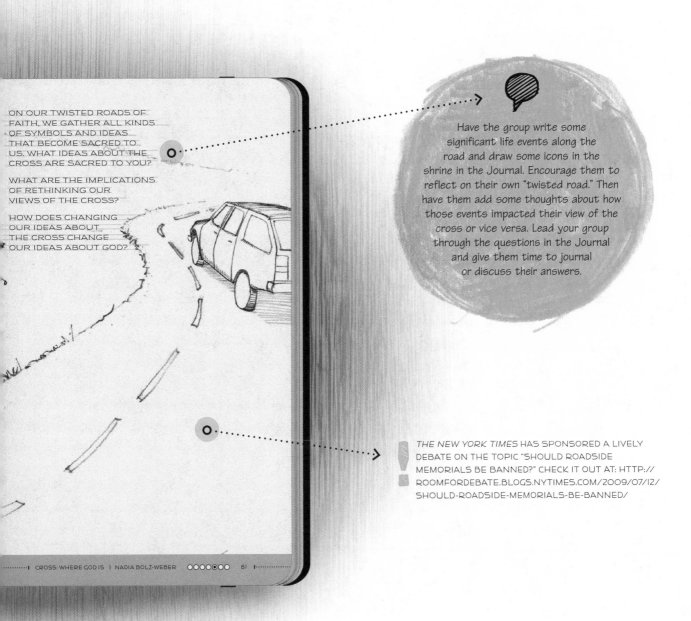

ON OUR TWISTED ROADS OF FAITH, WE GATHER ALL KINDS OF SYMBOLS AND IDEAS THAT BECOME SACRED TO US. WHAT IDEAS ABOUT THE CROSS ARE SACRED TO YOU?

WHAT ARE THE IMPLICATIONS OF RETHINKING OUR VIEWS OF THE CROSS?

HOW DOES CHANGING OUR IDEAS ABOUT THE CROSS CHANGE OUR IDEAS ABOUT GOD?

Have the group write some significant life events along the road and draw some icons in the shrine in the Journal. Encourage them to reflect on their own "twisted road." Then have them add some thoughts about how those events impacted their view of the cross or vice versa. Lead your group through the questions in the Journal and give them time to journal or discuss their answers.

THE NEW YORK TIMES HAS SPONSORED A LIVELY DEBATE ON THE TOPIC "SHOULD ROADSIDE MEMORIALS BE BANNED?" CHECK IT OUT AT: HTTP://ROOMFORDEBATE.BLOGS.NYTIMES.COM/2009/07/12/SHOULD-ROADSIDE-MEMORIALS-BE-BANNED/

CROSS: WHERE GOD IS | NADIA BOLZ-WEBER ○○○○◉○○ 81

The next session of animate focuses in on the Bible. While the cross is a powerful symbol, its power is drawn from the Gospel—the good news conveyed by way of the Scriptures. The Bible fills out our understanding of the cruciform life with the story of God's love for the world in Christ. Be sure to encourage the group to keep thinking, praying, and talking about the everyday significance of the cross by way of their interaction with the Journal and one another.

BIBLE | A BOOK LIKE NO OTHER
LAUREN WINNER

IS IT CRAZY FOR ME TO HOPE THAT THROUGH YEARS OF
REREADING THIS BIBLE I MIGHT ONE DAY GET TO SEE A BLUER SKY?

In the last session, Nadia revealed many views of God's relationship to the cross. Is God on it? Over it? Above it? What do our perceptions of the cross tell us about how we see God? In this session, Lauren Winner takes us into the Bible, God's Word. Lauren was slow to embrace the Bible but came to do so in new and different ways. As you work through this session, your group may find new and different ways to see scripture too.

LAUREN FOCUSES ON TRYING TO

answer a question many of us have probably asked at one point or another: Is the Bible worth reading over and over and over? Consider filling your room with books of all kinds. As people arrive, encourage them to peruse the book selection and choose a few favorites that they might read and reread. You might also choose to play some background music, such as "Word of God, Speak" by Mercy Me, "The B-I-B-L-E," or "Tell Me the Stories of Jesus."

IN THE FIRST SPREAD, THE ARTIST WANTS

us to contrast the task of searching scripture, a la Acts 17:10-12, with the popular notions of the Bible as a book of quick and easy answers. The result is a spread that's pretty dark. Consider providing some gel pens or whiteout pens for people to write, sketch, or doodle in their Journals.

The books that eventually made it into the Bible sometimes hint at what the "Word of God" is and does. Psalm 119:103-105; Isaiah 40:8,9; Hebrews 4:12; and 2 Timothy 3:16,17 are popular examples. Split these passages up among your group members and have them report what adjectives they find in each passage. Have a volunteer write those adjectives alongside the words your group came up with.
• How does our perception of the Bible compare to the descriptions Bible writers offer for "the Word of God"?
• If you could add to or change these texts about the Bible, would you? Why or why not?

IS THE BIBLE WORTH RE-READIN

animate

IN 2000, GALLUP DID A STUDY ON BIBLE USAGE. THEY FOUND
• 92% OF AMERICAN HOUSEHOLDS OWN A BIBLE
• 59% REPORT THAT THEY READ THE BIBLE OCCASIONALLY (DOWN FROM 73% IN THE MID-1980S)
• 37% SAY THEY READ THE BIBLE AT LEAST ONCE PER WEEK
IT SEEMS PEOPLE TEND TO OVERSTATE THEIR RELIGIOUS FAITHFULNESS. ACCORDING TO GALLUP, "DESPITE THE IMPRESSIVE STATISTICS CONCERNING BIBLE READING AND STUDY, IT IS APPARENT THAT IGNORANCE ABOUT ITS CONTENTS IS WIDESPREAD."

····> For more on this study, see the article, "Six in Ten Americans Read Bible at least Occasionally" on gallup.com.

HOW DO WE LIVE WITH SCRIPTURE IN A WAY THAT SHOWS THE WORDS ARE UNIQUE?

PASTOR KNOW-IT-ALL

LET ME TELL YOU WHAT THIS BAT-UH-BALL SAYS ABOUT...

over and over and over?

"THE CHURCH — AND THAT'S US; WE ARE THE CHURCH — THE CHURCH HAS GROPED FOR WAYS TO TALK ABOUT THE WAYS THE BIBLE REVEALS TO US WHO WE REALLY ARE — WE HAVE GROPED FOR WAYS TO TALK ABOUT ALL THE BIBLE CAN REAVEAL TO US ABOUT GOD AND GOD'S WORLD."
-LAUREN WINNER

BIBLE: A BOOK LIKE NO OTHER | LAUREN WINNER ⦿⦿⦿⦿⦿⦿ 89

Ask your group, "How do we live with scripture in a way that shows the words are unique?" Invite everyone to sketch a stock market-like graphic chart of his or her relationship with scripture. Have them label the change points such as confirmation, college, or other events. Some members might remember parents reading the Bible to them as a child. Others may flat-line straight through to the present. Compare responses. How does their variety of experiences, thoughts, and opinions allow more room for living with scripture?

The monk and pastor images provide quite the contrast. They suggest completely different approaches to the Bible. Brainstorm other images. Have a group member write the images on a whiteboard or chart paper. Keep an eye out for themes. Perhaps many of your group members find the Bible intimidating. Or maybe they see it as a contested book. Welcome all thoughts and opinions.
• Have you ever encountered someone who thought he or she knew everything about the Bible? How did you react?
• How do you think your perceptions of the Bible affect how you hear what it has to say?
• What would make the Bible easier to read and understand?

Read Lauren's quote. Lauren believes the church has groped for ways to keep the Bible central throughout history. Like Lauren gropes for her cat-eye glasses in the morning so she can see clearly, the church has groped for clarity through the Bible.
• How have you groped for clarity and direction in your life? How has the Bible interplayed with that experience?
• What adjectives would you use to describe your interactions with the Bible?
• How does the Bible reveal your purpose for being here on earth? Where else do you search for that purpose?

Lauren is unique among the animate theologians because she was not born and raised a Christian. She converted first to Orthodox Judaism and then to Christianity.
• How did you become a Christian?
• Have you ever explored other religions or beliefs? Why or why not?
• How do you think the experience of conversion might shape someone's attitudes about their new religion's sacred texts?
• How might you look at Christianity and the Bible differently if you were new to it? What traditions, teachings, or practices might you appreciate more? Which ones might strike you as a little odd?

LAUREN LOVES—AND NEEDS—HER MANY

pairs of cat-eye glasses. Looking at the Bible through different lenses, such as historical, literary, or devotional lenses, can provide different perspectives on the text. What lenses do you grope for in order to read the Bible? How about the members of your group?

Watch the video together.
Lauren struggles with why the church rereads the Bible over and over again. In some ways, she understands that rereading is good and important. She rereads some of her favorite novels and novellas once each year. But the church has reread the Bible endlessly for thousands of years.
• What favorite books do you reread?
• What kinds of books do you think are worth rereading again and again? Why?
• How does the Bible fit in? Do you reread it on your own or just hear it in church and Bible study? Why?
• If the Bible was split up into 66 separate books, which ones would you buy first and why?
• Why does Lauren think the Bible is worth rereading?
• What do you think about her reasons?

WHO IS LAUREN WINNER?

LAUREN BROKE ONTO TH
CHRISTIAN SCENE WITH HE
2000 BOOK, *GIRL MEETS GO*
IN WHICH SHE CHRONICLE
HER CONVERSION FIRST T
ORTHODOX JUDAISM, THE
TO CHRISTIANITY. SHE IS A
ASSISTANT PROFESSOR C
CHRISTIAN SPIRITUALITY A
DUKE DIVINITY SCHOOL

WHEN LAUREN FIRST STARTE
ATTENDING WEEKLY WORSH
SERVICES, SHE WAS STRUC
BY THE WAY THE CHURC
TREATED SCRIPTURE. SH
SAYS, "I FOUND IT STRANG
THAT WE KEPT READIN
THE SAME BOOK OVER AN
OVER AGAIN. WEEK AFTE
WEEK, YEAR AFTER YEA
THIS ENDLESS REREADIN
OF THIS ONE BOOK

LAUREN TRIVIA:
• BA FROM COLUMBIA UNIVERSITY
• MPHIL FROM CAMBRIDGE UNIVERSITY
• MDIV FROM DUKE DIVINITY SCHOOL
• PHD IN HISTORY FROM COLUMBIA
• FELLOW AT THE INSTITUTE OF SACRED MUSIC AT YALE UNIVERSITY
• OWNS 30 PAIRS OF CAT-EYE GLASSES
• DOESN'T OWN A TV
• READS. A LOT, A WHOLE LOT.
• WROTE HER DISSERTATION ABOUT CHRISTIAN PRACTICES IN 18TH CENTURY VIRGINIA
• DOESN'T USE SOCIAL MEDIA. AT ALL.

LAUREN'S BOOKS:
GIRL MEETS GOD
MUDHOUSE SABBATH
REAL SEX
STILL

THE BIBLE IS A COLLECTIO
AKA "CANON" OF 66 BOOK'S
ALMOST AS MANY AUTHOR

DUKE CHAPEL

• 90

A BIBLE "DAGWOOD" - YUM! CHIC YOUNG'S 1936-PRESENT CARTOON CHARACTER DAGWOOD BUMSTEAD WAS KNOWN FOR HIS OUTRAGEOUSLY ENORMOUS SANDWICH CREATIONS. SINCE THEN THE TERM "DAGWOOD" HAS BEEN APPLIED TO ANY NUMBER OF CRAZY CONCOCTIONS—LIKE THE BIBLE FOR INSTANCE. FOR A FUN SNACK, SUPPLY INGREDIENTS FOR THE GROUP TO MAKE THEIR OWN DAGWOOD SANDWICHES. TALK ABOUT WHAT THEY INCLUDED OR LEFT OUT. DON'T FORGET THE SKEWERED OLIVE THAT HOLDS IT ALL TOGETHER!

ERASMUS
DUTCH HUMANIST, REFORM-
MINDED CATHOLIC PRIEST,
SCHOLAR, LINGUIST.
IN 1516 PUBLISHED GREEK
NEW TESTAMENT WHICH
HE COMPILED FROM
ANCIENT MANUSCRIPTS.

DESIDERIUS
ERASMUS OF
ROTTERDAM
•1466-1536

"I TOLD PARSONS TO LEAVE
THEIR WRANGLINGS AND
READ THE BIBLE... I TOLD
POPES AND CARDINALS TO
LOOK AT THE APOSTLES,
AND MAKE THEMSELVES
MORE LIKE TO THEM."

THOMAS MERTON
TRAPPIST MONK, SPIRITUALIST, AUTHOR, POET

GREATEST HITS:
THE SEVEN STOREY MOUNTAIN
LIFE IN SOLITUDE
NEW SEEDS OF CONTEMPLATION

• A COMMITTED PACIFIST, MERTON
  PROTESTED THE VIETNAM WAR.
• LIVED AT THE ABBEY OF
  GETHSEMANI IN KENTUCKY
• BELIEVED SPIRITUALITY IS THE
  MYSTICAL UNION BETWEEN
  A HUMAN BEING AND GOD.
  SCRIPTURE HELPS US MAKE SENSE
  OF THAT UNION, BUT IT DOESN'T
  REPLACE OR CREATE THAT UNION.

THOMAS MERTON
• 1915-1968

"The BIBLE is ABUNDANT IN A WEIRD AND
UNIQUE WAY. I have come into that RICHER
UNDERSTANDING OF THE [BIBLE] NOT BY thinking
abstractly ABOUT IT, BUT BY ACTUALLY Living
WITH IT, READING it, PRAYING it,
and praying that I might become A PERSON WHO
CAN Hear its LIVELINESS." —Lauren Winner

Lauren quotes Erasmus, who said we
should celebrate the Bible in our daily lives.
Ask the group to brainstorm what it would mean
for them to sing scripture at their daily work or
take scripture into themselves in a wholly, bodily way.

Role-play a comedic scene at the office. Have two
people in your group sit in imaginary adjoining cubicles.
One worker is a normal and quiet person. The other
is a "sing while I plow" kind of Christian. Encourage
both to play their part enthusiastically.
• Do you think this is what Erasmus
  envisioned? Why or why not?
• What are some real ways you could celebrate
  scripture in your daily life? Make a list or
  sketch yourself in the Journal.

"THE BIBLE IS AN ACT OF FAITHFUL IMAGINATION, IT IS NOT
A PACKAGE OF CERTITUDES." —WALTER BRUEGGEMANN,
CONTEMPORARY OLD TESTAMENT SCHOLAR

Thomas Merton commented on
the relationship between scripture
and the experience of God. Scripture helps
us interpret and understand our experience
of God, but it cannot replace that experience.
Have the group think of times when they have
sensed God's presence or felt union with God.
• Did any of those moments come when
  you were reading scripture?
• Do you think you are more likely to experience
  God when reading scripture? Why or why not?
• If the Bible tells us about God but is not
  God itself, how does that affect why
  or how you read scripture?
• How does Merton's view of scripture
  compare to that of Erasmus?

THE PROCESS OF SELECTING WHICH

books went into the Bible is not without some controversy. Certain people suspect that the selection of books was dictated by an attempt to push minority theologies out. It's true that the birth of what we now call the Bible wasn't easy. Many imagine the process of canonization as a power play. Consider having some solid history about the process of canonization at your disposal to quickly respond to questions that come up.

THE BIBLE IS MADE UP OF STORIES, LAWS, PROPHECIES, SONGS, POEMS, NARRATIVES, PERSONAL LETTERS, AND APOCALYPTIC LITERATURE. OVER TIME, THE CHURCH STRUGGLED TO DETERMINE WHICH WRITINGS WERE WORTHY OF BEING IN THE CANON OR NOT. THAT INCLUDED 15 BOOKS KNOWN AS THE "INTER-TESTAMENTAL BOOKS," OR THE APOCRYPHA. THE CANON WAS SET AT 66 IN 1545 DURING THE COUNCIL OF TRENT. BUT EVEN THE ORIGINAL KING JAMES VERSION OF 1611 INCLUDED THE APOCRYPHA. THAT WAS TOSSED OUT OF PROTESTANT BIBLES FOR GOOD IN 1647 BY THE WESTMINSTER CONFESSION.

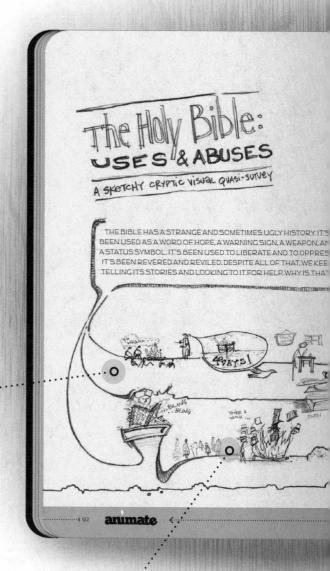

The Holy Bible: USES & ABUSES
A SKETCHY CRYPTIC VISUAL QUASI-SURVEY

THE BIBLE HAS A STRANGE AND SOMETIMES UGLY HISTORY. IT'S BEEN USED AS A WORD OF HOPE, A WARNING SIGN, A WEAPON, AND A STATUS SYMBOL. IT'S BEEN USED TO LIBERATE AND TO OPPRESS. IT'S BEEN REVERED AND REVILED. DESPITE ALL OF THAT, WE KEEP TELLING ITS STORIES AND LOOKING TO IT FOR HELP. WHY IS THAT?

animate

One of the most-cited reasons for people leaving the church is that they see the church as hypocritical. While Christians tout being welcoming and loving, many use the Bible as a defense for exclusion and hatred. Lauren refers to this part of the Bible's "ugly history." Look over the story lines of Bible uses and abuses together. Sketch in some other arguments you've heard in mainstream media or from people you know.
• Have you ever thought about leaving the church? Why or why not?
• How have you heard the Bible used to defend something good or bad?
• When have you referenced the Bible in an argument?
• What are some ways you could use the Bible for good?

THE STORY LINES INCLUDE IMAGES

of Bible study groups and storytellers, prophets and preachers, printing presses and digital readers, heretics and witches, even Paul and Jesus. But don't give all this away. Invite your group to surface what they see in the sketch and what it suggests both positively and negatively about the Bible.

For more information check out John Barton's *Holy Writings, Sacred Text: the Canon in Early Christianity*, (Louisville, Ky.: Westminster John Knox Press, 1998).

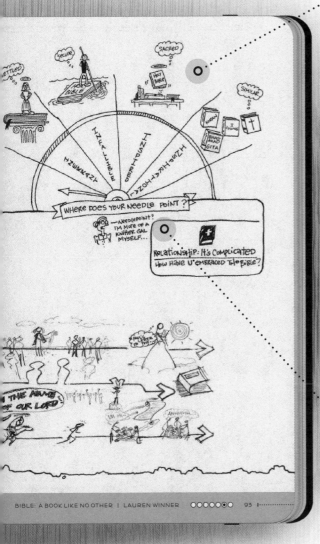

BIBLE: A BOOK LIKE NO OTHER | LAUREN WINNER ⭕⭕⭕⭕⭕⭕ 93

Share the definitions below with your group as they look at the Bible Meter:
Infallible: divinely dictated and therefore incapable of error
Inerrant: divinely given and not including errors
Inspired: God- or Spirit-assisted and human-written and therefore trustworthy
Inspirational: human-authored and with uplifting content
Have the group mark where they would place their own views on the meter.
• What has shaped your views of scripture?
• Why does your personal view of scripture seem logical to you?
• What happens when you debate scripture with someone who views it differently from you?
• Given the chance, how would you change the mainstream view of the Bible?

TALKING ABOUT SCRIPTURE CAN

raise many personal opinions from you and your group members. Some will be stronger than others. Because faithful people base beliefs and morals on their interpretation of the Bible, this book goes deep. Have a plan ready to deal with conflict and to direct conversations and debate in a healthy direction. Reading Jesus' words in John 13:34-35 and/or 17:20-21 together may help.

IN 2007, GALLUP SURVEYED AMERICANS ON HOW WE DEFINE THE BIBLE. THEY FOUND:
• 31% SEE THE BIBLE AS THE LITERAL WORD OF GOD
• 47% SEE IT AS INSPIRED BY THE WORD OF GOD
• 19% SEE IT AS A HUMAN COLLECTION OF FABLES, LEGENDS, AND HISTORY
THAT SURVEY COMBINES THE TWO CATEGORIES OF "INFALLIBLE" AND "INERRANT." FOR MORE INFORMATION, CHECK OUT "ONE-THIRD OF AMERICANS BELIEVE THE BIBLE IS LITERALLY TRUE" ON GALLUP.COM.

THE BIBLE BOOKS WE HAVE ARE ALL COPIES OF COPIES OF THE ORIGINALS. THE PROCESS OF TRANSMITTING THE ORIGINAL SCRIPTURE INTO THE BIBLES WE USE TODAY LEAVES ROOM FOR HUMAN ERROR AND EVEN HUMAN LICENSE. SOME RECENT SCHOLARS, LIKE BART EHRMAN OF THE UNIVERSITY OF NORTH CAROLINA, HAVE EVEN RAISED UP THE COPYISTS' FREEDOM TO UNDERMINE OVER-CONFIDENT FUNDAMENTALISTS.

Check out Bart Ehrman's book, *Mis-Quoting Jesus: The Story Behind Who Changed the Bible and Why* (New York: HarperOne, 2005). If you're interested, Stephen Colbert "debated" Bart Ehrman and his book in 2006. Watch the video here: http://www.colbertnation.com/the-colbert-report-videos/70912/june-20-2006/bart-ehrman.

RECENT RESEARCH HAS FOUND THAT PEOPLE ACTUALLY DO THINK DIFFERENTLY DEPENDING ON WHERE THEY ARE. THEY THINK BETTER WHEN THEY ARE LITERALLY "OUTSIDE THE BOX." WHERE WE DO OUR THINKING IMPACTS HOW WE THINK—IT'S CALLED "EMBODIED COGNITION."

LAUREN IS A PROFESSOR OF

Christian Spirituality, and she works hard not to just stay in her head. Take advantage of her very physical and creative Bible reading practices—try it in different places, on a hard-boiled eggs or cake, singing at the plow—to help you be creative with your group. You might even think of foods that could be fun or funny (Bible fortune cookies?) or places in your building that would enhance parts of the session. Go with it!

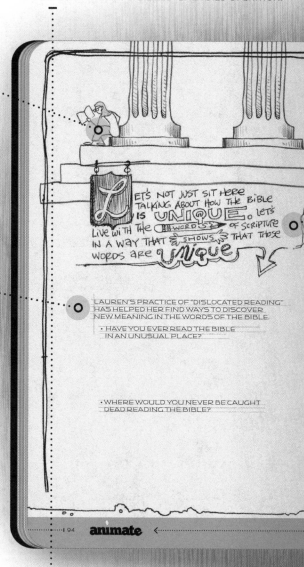

LET'S NOT JUST SIT HERE TALKING ABOUT HOW THE BIBLE IS UNIQUE. LET'S LIVE WITH THE WORDS OF SCRIPTURE IN A WAY THAT SHOWS THAT THOSE WORDS ARE UNIQUE

LAUREN'S PRACTICE OF "DISLOCATED READING" HAS HELPED HER FIND WAYS TO DISCOVER NEW MEANING IN THE WORDS OF THE BIBLE.

• HAVE YOU EVER READ THE BIBLE IN AN UNUSUAL PLACE?

• WHERE WOULD YOU NEVER BE CAUGHT DEAD READING THE BIBLE?

Have fun planning a "dislocated reading" strategy for this week. Work together to create a list of passages you could experience in unusual places. Allow time for your group to throw out ideas. Consider adding some of the following: Genesis 1, Daniel 6, Luke 23, Matthew 6:25-30, Mark 2:1-12 and 11:15-19, John 8:2-11, and Acts 16:25-40. Encourage your group to write a few other passages and ideas about where they might read them in their Journals.

• Where might you read some of these passages? Be creative! Radical, even.
• How do you think people will respond when they see you reading a Bible?
• How would you respond if you saw someone reading a Bible in a public place?

I 94   animate

THE BIBLE IS EVERYWHERE. THERE ARE BIBLES IN MOST HOTEL ROOMS ACROSS THE GLOBE, THANKS TO THE MINISTRY OF GIDEON INTERNATIONAL. THE BIBLE HAS BEEN TRANSLATED INTO OVER 2,000 LANGUAGES. IT IS THE BEST-SELLING BOOK IN HUMAN HISTORY BY A WIDE MARGIN. THE FIRST TRANSLATION OF THE BIBLE INTO ENGLISH CAME IN 1382 BY A GUY NAMED JOHN WYCLIF.

Check out the Op-Ed article, "When Truisms are True," at nytimes.com.

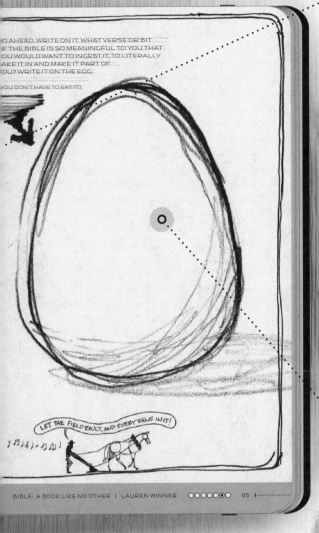

Have each person in the group
open the Bible randomly to a passage
and read the story or teaching silently.
Have group members engage their "faithful
imagination" and "live with the words of scripture."
Give people a chance to share their reactions. If
you have time, consider allowing group members
to go find a new place inside or outside your
meeting space to read their scripture passage.
• What did you discover about God or yourself?
• What do you feel called to do because
of this experience with scripture?
• How often do you feel the Bible
moving you to do something? How
often do you listen?

* THIS ACTIVITY IS A BIT
of a high-wire act. It is designed to
engage the imagination of your group.
Be ready for some strange passages!

! SCRIPTURE OFFERS MANY IMAGES OF PEOPLE
INTERNALIZING GOD'S WORD. IN EZEKIEL 2:1-4,
GOD ACTUALLY TELLS THE PROPHET TO EAT
THE SCROLL AND THEN TALK TO THE PEOPLE.
IN PSALM 119:11, THE PSALMIST PRAYS, "I HIDE/
TREASURE YOUR WORD IN MY HEART SO I MAY
NOT SIN AGAINST YOU." AND IN HIS LETTER
TO THE COLOSSIANS 3:16, PAUL WRITES, "LET
THE WORD OF GOD DWELL IN YOU RICHLY."

Many people can quote their
favorite scriptures. Other people aren't
as familiar with the text. Brainstorm some
favorite or well-known Bible verses. Then allow
time for group members to decorate their egg
with one. Encourage the group to comment
on their verses and to make notes around
the egg or in their Bibles. Launch them into
thinking about which scripture they would
pick to take into their bodies and why.
• How do you think a person who
has swallowed scripture
might behave?

"THIS IS SOMETHING ELSE WE DON'T DO WITH JANE
AUSTEN. WE DON'T CARVE PHRASES FROM HER
NOVEL INTO A HARDBOILED EGG AND EAT THEM FOR
BREAKFAST . . . BECAUSE, REALLY, YOU MIGHT LOVE
JANE AUSTEN. BUT YOU DON'T WANT TO TAKE HER
INTO YOURSELF WHOLLY, BODILY, IN QUITE THE SAME
WAY AS WE WANT TO FEED ON SCRIPTURE."

THERE'S A LOT OF FREE SPACE

on these pages for your group to gather their thoughts and jot down some ideas. Whether it's during your group time, immediately after, or on their own between this session and the next, offer group members the leisure and focus to ruminate on their relationship with the Bible. Not just what it's been but what it could be.

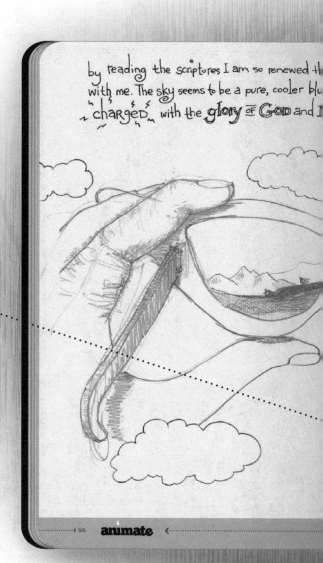

by reading the scriptures I am so renewed th_____ with me. The sky seems to be a pure, cooler blu_____ "charged" with the glory of GOD and I

I 96   animate

As Christians, scripture has the ability to make our path clearer and to help us more greatly appreciate the world around us. To illustrate how gray-scale the world is without scripture's lens, imagine a bland story like this one: *Once there was a guy who wanted a beautiful woman. Another guy wanted her too. Two tribes warred for years. Many people died. Pretty boring.* But that's the plot of Homer's *The Iliad*, without the gods invisibly moving the action forward. *The Iliad* is a classic that has captured human imagination for almost 3,000 years, but without the key ingredient—the gods—it's just a dull story.

- What does God-consciousness add to your experience of the world?
- Consider something you see everyday. How might you see it differently through scripture engaged by faith?
- What do you think Lauren sees in scripture through her cat-eye glasses that you could see if you approached it in a new way?

DON'T BE AFRAID TO SHARE

your own experiences with your group. When has the Bible made the sky more blue—or any other color for that matter? Tell your story! Show your group how to do this in a way that draws the conversation forward rather than defining what someone else should feel or be.

Other theologians and biblical interpreters use the image of the Bible as a lens through which we see God and the world more clearly. Two examples are George Lindbeck, *The Nature of Doctrine: Religion and Theology in a Postliberal Age*, (Louisville, Ky.: Westminster John Knox, 2009); and Marcus Borg, *Reading the Bible Again for the First Time*, (San Francisco: HarperSanFrancisco, 2002).

Thomas Merton's words are poetry. So is Lauren's question. Theology can be beautiful and artistic. Have your group describe the impact scripture has on their experience of the world in a way that speaks specially to them, whether it's artistically, musically, or in written word.
• "What is your version of seeing a bluer sky?
• What is it that God could do in you, through you, for you through the rhythm of Bible reading?"
• Sketch, color, or write in your Journal as you play with these questions.

WHAT KIND OF LEARNERS

do you have in your group? Artistic? Musical? Verbal? Collect supplies to appeal to everyone in your group. Some may want to sketch or paint on these pages. Others might add some poetry of their own. Still others might like to conclude this session with singing or prayer. Perhaps you want to have them explore Lauren's animating question with some between-session creativity. Make sure you're engaged in this activity to encourage others.

Lauren's glasses are a metaphor for the ways the Bible can improve our vision. We may honestly struggle with its contradictions and misuses, but it's a book Christians keep reading because of the radical worldview it offers: "See what love the Father has given us, that we should be called children of God; and that is what we are" (1 John 3:1). How will your group live with the Word?

leader NOTES

CHURCH | AN IMPERFECT FAMILY
BRUCE REYES-CHOW

WHEN WE CALL THE CHURCH A
FAMILY, DO WE REALLY MEAN IT?

This is the final session of animate | faith. In this session, Bruce Reyes-Chow addresses a question most of us have probably asked ourselves—why go to church? Bruce doesn't shy away from the downsides of church going, but he still asserts the value of being a part of a faithful community.

THE OPENING SECTION OF THE JOURNAL

sets up the question, "Why go to church?" Put up two sheets of chart paper in your meeting space. Title one "Why?" and the other "Why Not?" As people arrive, encourage your group to write reasons to go or not go to church. Invite them to add to the list at any time during the session.

AS YOU PREP FOR THIS SESSION,

think back through your history of going or not going to church. Be aware of your personal definition of church and its purpose. Think of times when church has and has not "done its job" in your life. This self-searching will prepare you to animate the conversation well.

WHAT FACTORS WEIGH IN ON YOUR DECISION TO GO TO CHURC

| 104   animate ◄

 Why go to church? Ask the group to share about times in their lives when they have or haven't been regular church attendees. Give them some time to jot a brief history of their churchgoing in their Journals. They can write the reasons they've gone to church near the church on the scale and the things that have drawn them away near the newspaper and coffee. Invite the group to share their responses.
• What's the make-up of our group—mostly regular or sporadic churchgoers? Or somewhere in between?
• Have you ever chosen not to go to church for a stretch of time? Why or why not?
• If you have left the church, what was the experience like and what brought you back?
• If you haven't, what has moved you to stay?

IN EVERY STUDY OF CHURCH ATTENDANCE, MORE OLD PEOPLE "DO" CHURCH THAN YOUNG, MORE WOMEN THAN MEN, MORE SOUTHERNERS AND UPPER-MIDWESTERNERS THAN NEW ENGLANDERS OR WESTERNERS, MORE BROWN-SKINNED PEOPLE THAN WHITE-SKINNED PEOPLE (PER CAPITA), AND MORE EVANGELICALS AND MORMONS THAN OTHER DENOMINATIONS.

For more information on this result, look up "Just Why Do Americans Attend Church?" from April 6, 2007, on gallup.com.

✳ YOU CAN REFLECT BRUCE'S AMBIVALENCE
about the institutional church visually in your room. Hang headlines
about clergy sex abuse, church tax fraud, declining attendance, and
so on in one section of your room. In another section, hang headlines
of church success stories like civil rights, charitable contributions,
educational advances, and AIDS care in Africa.

Read Bruce's quote together.
Even Bruce, who has had a career
in the church, has moments when
he doesn't think that church is the
best place to be a faithful person.
• How do you feel about Bruce's admission?
• Brainstorm some options for "expressing
and living out one's faith." How do these
compare to the church experience?
• How have your experiences within
a church helped you live out
your faith? How have they
hindered it?

"THE WAYS WE TRY TO MIMIC THE CULTURE OF PROSPERITY AND
CORPORATE LIFE; THE HYPOCRISY THAT WE EXUDE AROUND
ISSUES OF POVERTY AND SOCIAL JUSTICE; AND THE EMOTIONAL
AND SOMETIMES PHYSICAL DAMAGE WE SOMETIMES DO TO ONE
ANOTHER ALL ARE GOOD REASONS TO RUN AWAY FROM OUR
LOCAL CONGREGATIONS AS FAST AS WE CAN."
– BRUCE REYES-CHOW

NOT? ADD THEM TO THEIR RESPECTIVE SIDE OF THE SCALE.

CHURCH: AN IMPERFECT FAMILY | BRUCE REYES-CHOW ○○○○○◉○ |05 |

Why DO people go to church?
Why DON'T people go to church? Invite
members of your group to talk about their
individual church experiences. Then compare your
group's answers to the answers Gallup found in their
study. Is your group a statistical norm or an outlier?
• What churches have you belonged to?
Why did you choose those churches?
• Have you visited many churches other than
your own? If so, what drew you into that new
experience? What turned you off?
• Do you ever invite anyone to join you at
your church? Why or why not?
• Think about your social circle. Which friends go to
church and which don't? What do you think keeps
some of your friends away from church?
• What sometimes threatens to keep
you away from church?

❗ WHEN GALLUP ASKED AMERICANS TO TELL IN THEIR OWN WORDS WHY
THEY GO TO CHURCH, THE TOP SEVEN ANSWERS WERE SPIRITUAL
GROWTH AND GUIDANCE (23%), GROUNDING AND INSPIRATION
(20%), FAITH (15%), WORSHIP (15%), FELLOWSHIP/COMMUNITY (13%),
BELIEF IN GOD/RELIGION (12%), ROUTINE FROM CHILDHOOD (12%).

❗ GALLUP ASKED PEOPLE WHO DON'T ATTEND CHURCH WHY THEY DON'T. IN
THEIR OWN WORDS, THEY GAVE THESE TOP THREE REASONS: DON'T AGREE
WITH ORGANIZED RELIGION/WHAT THEY PREACH (24%), DON'T BELIEVE IN
GOING TO CHURCH (16%), AND CHURCHES ASK FOR TOO MUCH MONEY (3%).

Throughout this session, you'll see the "culture hearth" of the church portrayed. It's filled with pictures,
plaques, and memorabilia of what it means to be a part of the church. In the 1998, Pulitzer Prize winning
Guns, Germs, and Steel, author Jared Diamond defines "culture hearth" as a center of cultural development.

PREPARE FOR THE VIDEO BY

introducing Bruce Reyes-Chow. Look together at Bruce's bio. What kind of person chooses to plant a church, be the "Pope" of Presbyterians, and simultaneously ask the question, "Why go to church?"

Watch the video together.
When you have finished watching, ask the group to name a few things that really stood out to them. Use that brief conversation to get the content of the video back in the air.
• Bruce names a handful of ways that people think of church. What role does church play in your life?
• What do you think of Bruce's comparison of a church to a family?
• How do individual parts of your church (such as small groups, choirs, and individual mentors) seem like a family to you?
• Some families stick together through thick and thin. Others break up under strain. There are churches of both kinds. When and where have you experienced or heard about both these types of churches?

YOUR GROUP WILL BE TALKING MORE

about Bruce's metaphors, especially the metaphor of family, throughout this session. Touch on them here to recollect the video, but let this activity be more of an "anticipatory set" for more conversation to come than an in-depth treatment.

 Dr. Madelyn Hunter developed a popular teaching model in the late 20th century that coined the term "anticipatory set." This is defined as the "hook" that inductively connects students to the subject matter, focusing attention on the topic by relating it to the experiences of learners.

BRUCE CONFESSES THAT THERE ARE PLENTY OF MORNINGS WHEN HE SIMPLY DOESN'T WANT TO GO TO CHURCH. AND YET, HE GOES. FOR BRUCE, THE CHURCH, LIKE ANY FAMILY, IS A PLACE TO GROW AND BECOME WHO HE WAS MEANT TO BE.

INCREASINGLY, CHRISTIANS ARE ASKING WHAT MAKES THE CHURCH RELEVANT. WE WANT TO KNOW WHY IT'S WORTH THE TIME AND EFFORT TO BE PART OF SOMETHING THAT IS OFTEN DYSFUNCTIONAL AND EVEN HARMFUL. YET BRUCE SUGGESTS THAT BY RECLAIMING THE IDEA OF CHURCH AS FAMILY, WE CAN FIND WAYS TO EMBRACE BOTH THE PAINFUL AND THE BEAUTIFUL WAYS THAT CHURCH CHANGES US.

BRUCE TRIVIA:
• PLANTED MISSION BAY COMMUNITY CHURCH IN SAN FRANCISCO IN 2000
• STARTING AN ONLINE CHURCH IN 2012
• ELECTED AND SERVED FOR TWO YEARS AS MODERATOR OF THE 218TH GENERAL ASSEMBLY OF THE PRESBYTERIAN CHURCH USA. IT'S KIND OF LIKE BEING THE POPE ONLY WITHOUT THE SNAZZY HAT.
• SOCIAL MEDIA GURU
• BA IN ASIAN AMERICAN STUDIES, SOCIOLOGY, AND RELIGION FROM SAN FRANCISCO STATE UNIVERSITY
• MDIV FROM SAN FRANCISCO THEOLOGICAL SEMINARY.

CHURCH: AN IMPERFECT FAMILY | BRUCE REYES-CHOW ○○○○○● 107

Even though Bruce has been working in the church for many years, he still understands the struggle of deciding if it's worth it to go to church. But Bruce embraces the idea of church as family. Families aren't ever perfect, and churches aren't ever perfect. But the love you get from a family and a church makes it worthwhile to be a part of one.
• When has your church showed you love and support?
• When has your church been a little messy and dysfunctional?
• Of all of those things, what draws you to be a part of your faith community?
• Do you agree with Bruce's metaphor of church as family? Why or why not?

Even first-century Christians sometimes decided not to go to church. The book of Hebrews chides people who "neglect to meet together," then coaxes them to attend worship so they can "stir one another up to love and good works" (10:23-25 ESV). Then the author threatens people with the worst kind of consequences for not going to church—even eternal punishment (10:26-31). Have someone read out Hebrews 10:23-25.
• Why does the author want these Christians to meet together?
• Tell about a time you've felt stirred up to love one another and to do good works by the church. What was the impact of this experience?
• What role does church play in your life?

YOU'D THINK PEOPLE WOULD GO TO CHURCH WHEN THEY ARE ECONOMICALLY DEPRESSED AND STOP WHEN THEY ARE FAT AND HAPPY. FOR EXAMPLE, AFTER SEPTEMBER II, 2001, WORSHIP ATTENDANCE SURGED. BUT GALLUP FOUND THAT FROM 2008-2010, CHURCH ATTENDANCE WAS LOWEST IN 2008 IN THE DEPTHS OF RECESSION AND ROSE PARALLEL WITH THE ECONOMIC CONFIDENCE.

Look up this study: "Americans' Church Attendance Inches Up in 2010" on gallup.com.

They say beauty is only skin deep. Can the same be said of the Body of Christ, the church? Ask the group which of the churches on this page they are initially attracted to and why.
- What might be the upsides of attending such a church?
- What might be the downsides?
- What value do you place on the physical structure of the church? Why?

"CHURCH" WAS DEFINITELY THE PEOPLE AND NOT A BUILDING FOR THE EARLIEST CHRISTIANS. THEY MET IN EACH OTHER'S HOUSES. SO WHEN THE APOSTLE PAUL TRIES TO GIVE ONE MAIN PURPOSE FOR WORSHIP IN 1 CORINTHIANS 12—14, HE WRITES ABOUT WORKING FOR "THE COMMON GOOD" (12:7) AND "BUILDING (ONE ANOTHER) UP" (14:4, 5, 26).

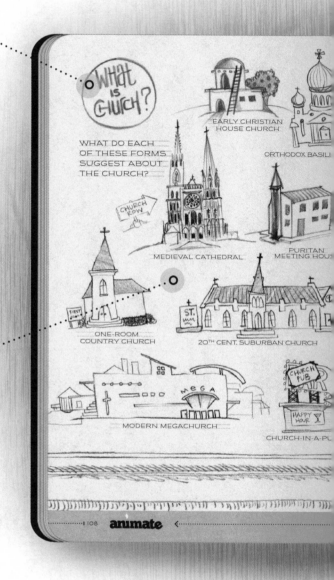

The kind of church we attend and the roles we play in it strongly impact our church experience. Bruce has played a variety of roles in differing church settings, from planting a church to holding the top position in the Presbyterian Church, one of the largest mainline denominations in the United States. Now he's starting an online church, a whole new kind of Christian community. Ask your group to inventory the kinds of churches they've attended. Then have them define the roles they played or are playing in each.

JESUS HAD A NUMBER OF CONVERSATIONS ABOUT THE SACRED SPACES. HIS CONVERSATION WITH THE WOMAN AT THE WELL GOT TO THE HEART OF WORSHIP (JOHN 4:19-26). HIS PREDICTION ABOUT THE TEMPLE CAME UP AT HIS TRIAL (MATTHEW 26:57-68), AND HE WAS EVEN CONNECTED WITH A BIT OF RENOVATION ACTIVITY (MATTHEW 27:50-54). JESUS BOTH ATTENDED PUBLIC WORSHIP (JOHN 7:10-18) AND REGULARLY TOOK PERSONAL TIME TO COMMUNE WITH GOD (LUKE 11:1).

✳ ## BRUCE IDENTIFIES THE GOD-CENTERED

nature of church as what distinguishes it, but there's a strong tension between the God-centered church and the benefits of church to a person, right? Turn the conversation in your group toward how they coexist.

Pose this question to your group. Invite them to imagine the ideal church together. Include a building, groups, programs, and even a description of the kinds of people who will attend.
• What is most important architecturally?
• What is most important programmatically?
• Where would your building be?
• What would happen in it?
• What would your group do outside it?
• How would you characterize this ideal church to people you meet? If you "build it," would these people come? Why? Then encourage the group to sketch out their ideal of church on this page—either in images or words. Follow up with the second question. Call out the unique features of each design and talk about the reasons behind each design.
•How can you apply some of these ideas to your church now?

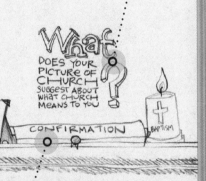

THE ARCHITECTURE OF A CHURCH REFLECTS THE STYLE OF THE DAY, BUT IT ALSO REFLECTS WHAT PEOPLE THOUGHT ABOUT THE FUNCTION OF THE CHURCH—WHO HAD THE AUTHORITY, WHO WAS WELCOME, WHAT ROLE THE CHURCH PLAYED IN A COMMUNITY.

WHEN YOU THINK OF A CHURCH, WHAT DO YOU SEE? SKETCH IT HERE

What DOES YOUR PICTURE OF CHURCH SUGGEST ABOUT WHAT CHURCH MEANS TO YOU

NEW MEMBER ORIENTATION   CONFIRMATION   BAPTISM

CHURCH: AN IMPERFECT FAMILY | BRUCE REYES-CHOW   ○○○○○●   109

The Apostle Paul pictures church as a place where people of diverse gifts each bring what they've got—a voice of wisdom, words of knowledge, special faith, the ability to heal, miraculous powers, prophetic powers, discernment, languages, and so on (1 Corinthians 12:1-11) Have someone read out 1 Corinthians 12:4-7 and 14:1-5, 26. Have the group listen for the way Paul pictures the purpose of the church meetings in Corinth. Ask people to name the purposes.
• When have you felt like you were contributing to the common good of the church?
• When have you been "built up" by a church gathering?
• When have you felt like you've helped "build up" others?
• How might all these themes of building up be understood as "God-centered?" See Ephesians 4:11-16.

✳ ## NOTE HOW THE "MANTLE" HOLDS

some church souvenirs: a confirmation certificate, baptism candle, and welcome photo. Urge the group to share some of their milestone moments in the church. But be sure to provide some explanation if the insider language goes over the head of anyone in the group who hasn't had such moments.

SOME LEADING THEOLOGIANS OF OUR TIME HAVE RECENTLY ASSERTED THAT ANY SELF-SERVING MOTIVE IS INCONGRUOUS WITH WORSHIP. PROFESSOR EMERITUS DAVID KELSEY IS AN EXAMPLE. HE IDENTIFIES THE CHURCH'S PRIMARY FUNCTION AS *DOXOLOGY*—A CELEBRATION OF GOD'S GLORY.

➤ David Kelsey, *Eccentric Existence: A Theological Anthropology* (2 Vols, Westminster John Knox Press, 2009); Miroslav Volf.

IN THE VIDEO, BRUCE DECONSTRUCTS SOME COMMON CHURCH METAPHORS.

Which of these metaphors speak—both positively and negatively—to your group? Engage members in the questions that the Journal provides and encourage them to list the values and limits of each one in their Journal.

Club, classroom, sporting event, theater, hospital, or family? All of the above? None of the above? Have the group reflect on the actual, on-the-ground, non-theoretical, lived-out purpose of their church. Does your church have a vision or mission statement? If so, does your experience line up with that stated purpose? Encourage them to think anthropologically. If you only had your experience to draw on, what would you say is the purpose of the church?

As part of his life in the church, Bruce has many visions for changing and growing the church. Take the group to http://reyes-chow.com/2012/02/new-presbyterian-church/.
• What's Bruce's new blueprint for the church?
• How do you understand these key points of Bruce's vision for his new church:
  Spiritual and Religious
  Gracious and Progressive
  Reformed and Presbyterian
  Open and Sourced
  Inward and Outward . . . but mostly outward
  Where we do it all through the lens of the life, death and resurrection of Jesus Christ.
• Should any of these points apply to your church? Why or why not?

WHO IS CHURCH?

BRUCE MENTIONS A HANDFUL OF METAPHORS FOR THE CHURCH:
+ A SOCIAL CLUB
+ A CLASSROOM
+ A SPORTING EVENT
+ A THEATER
+ A HOSPITAL

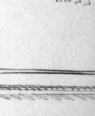

WHY DO THESE STICK AROUND?

WHAT MAKES THEM WORK?

WHAT ARE THEIR LIMITS?

HOW DOES BRUCE'S METAPHOR OF CHURCH AS FAMILY WORK? IS IT TOO CLICHÉD?

animate

THE FIRST Q&A IN THE WESTMINSTER SHORTER CATECHISM IS: Q: "WHAT IS THE CHIEF END OF MAN?" A: "MAN'S CHIEF END IS TO GLORIFY GOD AND ENJOY HIM FOREVER." KEEP IN MIND THIS IS A DIRECT QUOTATION OF THE HISTORIC DOCUMENT. YOU MAY WANT TO MAKE GENDER LANGUAGE MORE INCLUSIVE.

Émile Durkheim, renowned sociologist and anthropologist, saw religion as the repository of cultural ideals. Churches, therefore, serve as "collective representations" of a community's values and aspirations. He wrote: "A religion is a unified system of beliefs and practices relative to sacred things, i.e., things set apart and forbidden—beliefs and practices which unite in one single moral community, called a Church, all those who adhere to them" (*The Elementary Forms of the Religious Life*, Book 1, Ch. 1).

"See all the people." That sounds simple enough; but who are those people? What does it mean to see them? Post these statements of Christian purpose around the room.
• Dietrich Bonhoeffer wrote in one of his Letters and Papers from Prison, "Jesus Christ is there only for others ... The church is only the church when it exists for others."
• William Temple, the Archbishop of Canterbury (1942–44), wrote, "The church is the only society in the world that exists for the benefit of those who are not its members."
• St. Teresa of Avila (1515–82) characterized church this way: "Christ has no body now on earth but yours. No hands but yours. No feet but yours. Yours are the eyes through which Christ looks out compassion on the world." Talk about the message of these quotations. Ask the group how the issue of church would change if it changed from being a place people go to a movement that embodies God's love in the world.

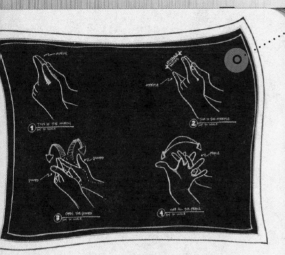

THE BIBLE OFFERS SOME METAPHORS AS WELL

+ THE BODY OF CHRIST (1 CORINTHIANS 12:12-27)
+ VINE AND BRANCHES (JOHN 15:5)
+ BRIDE OF CHRIST (EPHESIANS 5:25-27)
+ WHERE TWO OR MORE ARE GATHERED (MATTHEW 18:20)
+ THE LIVING TEMPLE (EPHESIANS 2:17-22)

WHAT DO THESE TELL YOU ABOUT THE WAY EARLY CHRISTIANS THOUGHT ABOUT CHURCH?

CHURCH: AN IMPERFECT FAMILY | BRUCE REYES-CHOW ○○○○○○● III

THE CLASSIC NURSERY RHYME DEPICTED IN THE JOURNAL HAS RECENTLY BEEN CHALLENGED BY FREDERICK W. SCHMIDT OF SOUTHERN METHODIST IN HIS *WASHINGTON POST* ONLINE ARTICLE "HERE IS THE CHURCH, HERE IS THE STEEPLE, OPEN THE DOORS AND..." (HTTP://ONFAITH.WASHINGTONPOST.COM/ONFAITH/PATHEOS/2010/09/HERE_IS_THE_CHURCH_HERE_IS_THE_STEEPLE_OPEN_THE_DOORS_AND.HTML).

Read together the passages connected to the metaphors in the Journal. Have the group also write in "CHURCH AS FAMILY (MARK 3:31-35)."
• What do these metaphors tell you about the way early Christians thought about the church?
• How do these metaphors help us understand what church is and how it functions in the world today?
• How does Brian McLaren's warning about the limitations of metaphors for God in Session 1 come into play in this session? When do our metaphors for the church fall short?
• The 15th century Protestant reformers urged Christians to distinguish between the "visible church," which is full of hypocrisy and corruption, and the "invisible church," which "is actually in God's presence," as John Calvin put it. In what ways is that distinction still relevant when talking about church?

A fuller version of Calvin's definition of the "invisible church" reads: "that which is actually in God's presence, into which no persons are received but those who are children of God by grace of adoption and true members of Christ by sanctification of the Holy Spirit ... [It] includes not only the saints presently living on earth, but all the elect from the beginning of the world" (Institutes 4.1.7).

Work this metaphor of family. Have the group reflect through sketching or writing in and around the frame in their Journals on their experience of family and how it helps or does not help them understand what the church is.
• What things would you do for family that you wouldn't do for anyone else?
• Does the same hold for your commitment to churchgoers? Why or why not?

BRUCE STAYS IN THE FAMILY OF CHURCH BECAUSE, HE SAYS, "IT'S THAT ACCEPTANCE, THAT LOVE, AND THAT CHALLENGE TO GROW THAT KEEPS ME COMING BACK TO CHURCH." AND BECAUSE OF HIS CHILDREN. "MORE OFTEN THAN NOT, IT'S A PLACE WHERE THEY WILL BE LOVED, THEY WILL BE ACCEPTED, AND THEY WILL GROW MORE AND MORE INTO THE PEOPLE GOD INTENDED THEM TO BE."

It's been said, "You can choose you friends, but you can't choose your family."
• How does this apply to your church family, especially given the splintering tendencies that Protestants are known for?
• How is God going to help our church become the church God imagines us to be?
• What part will I play in that happening?

MARTIN LUTHER POSTED HIS "95 THESES" ON THE DOOR OF THE CASTLE CHURCH IN WITTENBERG IN 1517. SINCE THAT TIME, PROTESTANTS HAVE SOMETIMES DECIDED THAT WE AREN'T OBLIGED TO TRY TOO HARD TO STAY TOGETHER. WE HAVE THE PROTESTING GENE, SO THE CHRISTIAN FAMILY TREE HAS A WHOLE LOT OF BRANCHES! THERE ARE CURRENTLY MORE THAN 33,000 CHRISTIAN DENOMINATIONS IN THE WORLD. THIS IS DUE IN PART TO THE FACT THAT WHEN THINGS DON'T GO OUR WAY, WE TEND TO TAKE OUR BALL AND GO HOME.

HURCH: AN IMPERFECT FAMILY | BRUCE REYES-CHOW ○○○○○○◉ 113 ⊢....

As you send out your group, encourage them to journal in the coming days about their church experiences. Perhaps suggest that they visit an unfamiliar church or two in the coming weeks, either on a Sunday morning or just for fun during the week. When they encounter a church, have them record it in their Journals along with some first impressions. What is that church? Why does that church exist? Can you tell from the building? The people walking in and out? The website? Check them out!

OUR SEVEN PRESENTERS IN THIS SERIES REPRESENT A STRANGELY WIDE SWATH OF CHRISTIAN DIVERSITY, INCLUDING ONE NONTRADITIONAL CHURCH IN EACH TIME ZONE! EACH ONE OFFERS A UNIQUE PERSPECTIVE ON THE CHURCH AND ITS MEMBERSHIP.

BRIAN MCLAREN—EAST-COAST EMERGENT: SEES CHURCH MEMBERS AS PEOPLE WHO ARE ON A SHARED QUEST BOTH WITH AND TOWARD GOD.

LILLIAN DANIEL—UNITED CHURCH OF CHRIST: ASSERTS THAT THE CHURCH KEEPS US ROOTED TO SOMETHING BIGGER THAN OURSELVES.

MARK SCANDRETTE—WEST COAST EMERGENT CHURCH AND EXPERIMENTAL COMMUNITY: HAS COME TO EXPECT THE CHURCH TO INSPIRE AND EQUIP US TO PRACTICE THE WAY OF JESUS.

SHANE HIPPS—MIDWEST EMERGENT: CHALLENGES THE CHURCH TO WORK OUT THE SIGNIFICANCE OF OUR SALVATION IN THE HERE AND NOW.

NADIA BOLZ-WEBER—ROCKY MOUNTAIN EMERGENT: BELIEVES THAT THE CHURCH'S ANCIENT ART, LITURGY, AND SYMBOLISM STILL HAS A LOT TO SAY.

LAUREN WINNER—EPISCOPALIAN AND PROFESSOR AT A METHODIST UNIVERSITY: HAS COME TO SEE GREAT VALUE IN CHURCH'S SURPRISING PRACTICE OF BIBLE "REREADING."

BRUCE REYES-CHOW—PRESBYTERIAN AND "PLANTING" AN ONLINE CHURCH: IT MAY BE MESSY, BUT FEELS THAT THE CHURCH IS STILL, ESSENTIALLY, FAMILY.

THE POINT: THERE ARE MANY WAYS TO BE AND DO CHURCH WELL.

The first leg of your group's animate journey is drawing to a close. Take an inventory of ideas, thoughts, and attitudes of your group. What new things have they had a chance to explore? What new ideas do they have about how to interact with the life of the church? Encourage members to continue interacting with their Journals and putting into practice some of the ideas of the animate™ theologians.

NOTES